BRISTOL'S FLOATING HARBOUR: THE FIRST 200 YEARS

Bristol's Floating Harbour: The first 200 years

Peter Malpass and Andy King

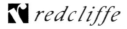 redcliffe

First published in 2009 by Redcliffe Press Ltd.,
81g Pembroke Road, Bristol BS8 3EA

www.redcliffepress.co.uk
info@redcliffepress.co.uk

ISBN 978-1-906593-28-5

The publishers are pleased to have worked with Bristol's Museums,
Galleries & Archives and the University of the West of England, Bristol in
this commemoration of the 200th anniversary of the Floating Harbour

British Library Cataloguing in Publication Data
A catalogue record for this book is available from the British Library

Design and typesetting by Steve Leary, steve@stevedesign.plus.com
Printed by HSW Print, Tonypandy

Acknowledgements

We are grateful to colleagues at Bristol's Museums, Galleries & Archives
(particularly Sheena Stoddard and David Emeney) and staff at the Bristol
Local Studies library for their help in locating material used in the book.
Thanks are also due to Kevin Pomeroy, Docks Engineer, who provided
valuable technical information about mud! Thanks also to all those who
have made comments on drafts of various chapters - we hope we have
learned from them.

CONTENTS

FOREWORD

For so significant an element of Bristol's economic, cultural and social life, it's surprising that so little has been written about the Floating Harbour. Bristol Museums, Galleries and Archives service has had a long association with the Harbour since opening the Industrial Museum there in 1978, and has continued custodianship of the historic railway, ships and cranes associated with it. I am therefore very pleased that we have been able to facilitate this new history, based on the unrivalled collections of archives, prints, paintings and photographs that the service holds for the public and the knowledge of the museums' staff and our partners from the University of the West of England.

M-Shed, the Industrial Museum's former home, is currently being transformed to be a new museum which will tell the city's rich story. The port has been a constant and evolving element of the city's development, and the new museum will reflect that fascinating, dynamic history, whilst also stimulating dialogue and debate to help shape the future of the city.

Kate Brindley

Director of Museums, Galleries & Archives
Bristol City Council

Opposite: The extent of the Floating Harbour in 1950

Woodpulp from Finland being discharged by crane into barges at Prince's Wharf, June 1954, for onward transportation through the Harbour to St Anne's Board Mills. (PBA 2387)

Bristol's Floating Harbour: the first 200 years

1 Introduction

In the past thirty years Bristol has been one of many cities around the world to put redundant port facilities at the heart of ambitious urban regeneration projects. Huge amounts of investment transformed the harbourside area, continuing a process that has brought back to life abandoned buildings and spaces. Recurrent renewal is a constant theme in the life of cities, and the bicentenary of Bristol's Floating Harbour in 2009 is a reminder that the current renaissance is only the latest – albeit the most profound – transformation to affect the area. It will not be the last. What people will do in and around the harbour over the next 200 years will undoubtedly change in ways we can barely imagine. The citizens who celebrated the opening of the Floating Harbour with a feast in May 1809 could not have foreseen how a project carried out for purposes appropriate to that time, could be recycled and reinvented for entirely different purposes in

the twenty-first century. The Floating Harbour remains a unique part of Bristol's urban landscape and a defining feature of the city, more vibrant and alive now than for many years. Thus in writing about the Floating Harbour we are conscious that we are looking at the first 200 years of a continuing and evolving story.

Bristol is a city of two rivers, the Avon and its smaller tributary the Frome. The original port was on the Avon, close to Bristol Bridge, but in the 1240s a great piece of medieval civil engineering created a wide and deep trench more than half a mile long, re-routing the Frome and establishing the famous Broad Quay as the heart of the port for the next 500 years. The construction of the Floating Harbour in 1804-09 transformed the tidal rivers into a harbour where ships remained afloat at the quayside whatever the state of the tide outside the locks, hence the name 'floating harbour'. The Harbour is a large

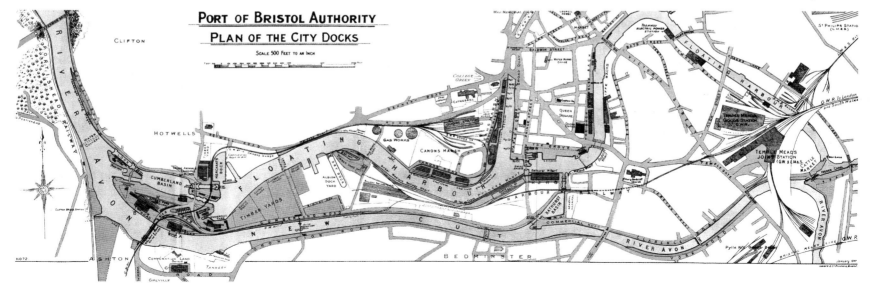

area of water, extending to more than 80 acres, snaking for two miles through the middle of Bristol from Temple Meads in the east to Rownham in the west. It follows the natural course of the river Avon together with the stretch of the river Frome that was dug out by hand in the mid-thirteenth century and is now known as St Augustine's Reach. The water within the Floating Harbour is held at the level of normal high tide by a system of locks and dams.

The construction works completed in 1809 served only to keep ships afloat but this was an important (if unintended) pre-condition for the subsequent development of a modernised industrial-era port, capable of accommodating far more ships, and surrounded by massive warehouses, transit sheds, steam (later electric) cranes, railway lines and goods yards. The transformation in train today is actually more radical than when the Floating Harbour was first constructed, because then it was all about enhancing and developing the traditional functions of the port, allowing it to work better in changed times. Now the transformation is about reinventing the Floating Harbour and the surrounding area as a completely different kind of space. It has become a part of the city where cargo liners, tramp steamers and lighters have given way to yachts, launches and houseboats. Most of the buildings around the water have changed over the years, with houses and apartment blocks replacing sheds and warehouses, although some landmarks such as the churches of St Stephen and St Mary Redcliffe remain from medieval times, along with the fine terraces of Georgian houses at Redcliffe Parade. Other buildings previously associated with port activities have been converted into offices, bars and restaurants. No longer a place where hundreds of men carry great planks of wood on their shoulders or heave barrels of wine or sacks of grain, the Floating Harbour is now primarily a place for relaxation. For the majority of visitors it is associated not with hard manual labour but with leisure, recreation and culture. In the present transition the name Harbourside is increasingly being used instead of the older Floating Harbour or City Docks. The language reflects and reinforces the change of emphasis

from the water to the land around it.

Much has been written about the history of Bristol, and inevitably, given the importance of the port in the city's past rise to prominence and prosperity, many authors refer at least in passing to the Floating Harbour.[1] Several accounts focus on the port in the period since 1800.[2] Biographies of I K Brunel routinely refer to his involvement with the Floating Harbour through his role as consultant engineer to the Dock Company between 1832 and 1852 and his two great steam ships built in Bristol.[3] Bristol is also discussed in general histories of ports in Great Britain.[4] Our purpose is partly to provide a new and up to date account for the bicentenary, and partly to offer a different interpretation which questions and challenges aspects of the conventional explanation of the course of events. We also want to set the story of the Floating Harbour in a broader national context.

There is a standard narrative of the history of the Floating Harbour up to the end of the nineteenth century. According to this view, which was undoubtedly influenced by Bristol's decline from its briefly held eighteenth-century position as the second city by size after London, and also the second largest port, the story is unremittingly negative. There was certainly unconscionable delay in building the Floating Harbour, the construction costs were double the original estimate and the Dock Company charged with managing the port was inefficient, ineffective and irresolute. Bristol was said, as a result, to be the most expensive port in the country, and trade was inevitably diverted elsewhere. Failure to develop the port facilities led, according to this view, to the loss of important and lucrative business to Liverpool in the 1840s, particularly transatlantic mail and passenger traffic. Then later in the century there was a long and damaging struggle over the issue of 'dockisation' (proposals to dam the Avon nearer its mouth to create a port capable of taking the largest ships then afloat) and schemes for new docks at the mouth of the river. Although Bristol was connected by rail to London from 1841 and to the rest of the country by the 1850s, the railway terminated at Temple Meads and did not reach the Floating Harbour until 1872. It was not until 1906,

Quay Head in 1826. (T. Rowbotham BMG Mb 6254)

The west end of Redcliffe Parade, showing the entrance gates to Bathurst Basin, 1827. (T. Rowbotham BMG M2934)

virtually 100 years after the completion of the Floating Harbour, that the harbour railway system was completed (and it never did connect to the ancient quays).

We want to develop a more positive perspective, which recognises that while Bristol declined relative to Liverpool and Glasgow in terms of population and volume of trade, it nevertheless continued to grow in absolute terms. The most remarkable feature of the history of the port of Bristol is surely not its decline but its survival, facilitated by the construction of the Floating Harbour. Bristol was a highly improbable place for a successful modern port, its ancient quays being eight miles up a small, winding and highly tidal river. The difference between high and low water at the entrance to the Floating Harbour is normally about 30 feet, more at spring tides. This is the highest tidal range found at any British port and has often been cited as a major drawback, but the tidal nature of the Avon must be seen as the main reason for there being a port at Bristol at all. The tide converts what is naturally a small and insignificant river into a channel capable of floating ships the size of the *Great Britain*, 300 feet in length. In the days of sail the incoming tide provided the propulsive power to carry ships inland as far as the lowest convenient bridging point. The daily sequence of tides also helps to scour the river, preventing it from silting up and suffering the fate of former river ports such as Chester and Norwich, both of which became unsustainable several hundred years ago. But the tides also became a source of difficulty for the port, hence the need to build some sort of floating harbour. Ships could only enter and leave the river when the tide was right. Once in port there were problems of loading and unloading as ships rose and fell with the tide. Generally they would settle comfortably into the mud at low tide, but sometimes they would tip over at dangerous angles as the water retreated, making it risky or even impossible to move cargo around. If a fire broke out it could easily spread rapidly through wooden ships crowded together and immovable for hours at a time.

The Floating Harbour certainly did cost a huge amount to build, but it was an ambitious and unique project, which provided an elegant and effective long-term solution to problems that had been debated for decades. It enabled the city docks to continue to operate commercially for over 150 years, despite massive changes in ship design, construction and propulsion, along with important changes in cargoes and cargo handling techniques. It was designed for short, broad, wooden sailing ships, but within fifty years it was accommodating the new generation of long, slender ships made of iron and powered by steam. The entrance locks had to be modified but the basic design of the Floating Harbour remained (and remains) intact. The creation of the Floating Harbour was an audacious piece of civil engineering, conceived before the development of modern techniques for modelling the complex movements of tidal and river water, and carried out with only the most primitive steam-powered technology. The construction of docks for loading and unloading was then a relatively new idea, and it was not generally accepted as the obvious way forward. Pioneering wet docks on the Avon, at Sea Mills (1712) and Champion's Dock at Rownham (1763), were not commercially successful, largely because they were felt to be too far from the city centre. Liverpool and Hull had already completed their first docks, and the first enclosed dock in London – the West India Dock – was opened in 1802. The engineer on that project was William Jessop, who went on to take responsibility for the Floating Harbour.

In that context, the Floating Harbour should be seen as a great success, and actually more successful than other docks constructed around that time. First, with 83 acres of enclosed water it was very much larger than the docks of Liverpool or London at the time of its completion; second, its long thin shape proved to be better for loading and unloading, especially as ships became larger. The first excavated docks tended to be square, following the precedents of earlier basins designed for laying-up rather than cargo handling. A square shape was ideal for laying-up idle ships, but loading and unloading required maximum lengths of quayside space, and so later dock design tended to favour longer and thinner shapes. Third, the

Floating Harbour retained and gave a new lease of life to the existing quays, seen at the time as a real benefit to the merchants whose offices, warehouses and trading networks were located there.

The Floating Harbour was also quite different in conception from other dock projects of that time. In general docks were being created in places like London and Liverpool either by digging out great holes in the ground next to the river or the sea shore, or by reclamation enclosing part of the sea. But in the case of the Floating Harbour the solution was the opposite: the harbour was created not primarily by excavation but by damming the river. The major excavation work was not in the harbour itself but in the construction of a new course for the river, making a tidal by-pass round the harbour. This had the advantage of minimising the disruption of the working of the port during construction.

The Floating Harbour differed from enclosed docks in other ways too. Its quays remained open and accessible, not closed off behind high walls. And the Floating Harbour was always more than a port in the sense that there were parts of the waterfront devoted to activities other than the loading and unloading of ships. Ship building, for example, continued in the Harbour right up to the 1970s. There were sites used primarily for processing and manufacturing, such as the Canon's Marsh Gas Works, the flour mills at Redcliffe Back and Finzel's huge sugar refinery at Counterslip on Temple Back. These plants may have used the water as a way of moving materials in and out, but in principle they were no different from similar businesses in different locations. It is also important to say that the Floating Harbour differed from the docks being built in London and Liverpool in that the extent of the ponded area of water in Bristol was a reflection of the best place to locate the dam, rather than an attempt to create a working dock of those dimensions.

Our account of the history of the Floating Harbour is structured around the idea of four transformations, cross-cut by four themes that run throughout the chronological narrative. The construction work of 1804-9 brought about the first transformation, converting what was essentially still a medieval tidal port into a floating harbour. This was the first major improvement to the port infrastructure since the digging of the new course of the Frome more than 550 years previously. Its impact on people working at the port must have been immense. Suddenly they were released from the age-old rhythm of the tidal river. Admittedly, ships could only enter and leave the harbour when the tide was right, but once inside they could be worked not only at will but also more safely and efficiently.

The construction of the Floating Harbour was an important transformation, but a limited one, which did not extend to improving the facilities within the harbour. Over the centuries there had been some small-scale extensions to the quays, but port activity was effectively confined to the stone quay that, by the 1790s, ran continuously from the Stone Bridge (opposite the bottom of Small Street) right round to Bristol Bridge. Elsewhere the banks of the Avon remained in a largely natural state, bordered by fields on the Bedminster side and on the north bank, below the Cathedral. Constructing the Floating Harbour did nothing to change this and it seems that no-one at that time had any plans to develop the port any further, and there was certainly no sign of any money for new projects. However, what had been conceived as a job done turned out to be only a pre-condition for the second transformation: the subsequent development of port facilities in response to economic and technological changes over the ensuing decades, resulting in a port for the industrial era dominated by iron and steel steamships. It was not until the 1860s that this second transformation began to gather momentum as new wharves were developed, railways were laid, a series of giant warehouses was built and powered cargo-handling cranes were introduced. Even then, many goods were man-handled on and off ships. It was in this period that the centre of gravity within the harbour began to move away from the ancient quays, downstream towards Wapping and the Cumberland Basin.

The third transformation came quite suddenly. The city docks experienced a period of prosperity after 1945 but by the late 1960s

Tombs's Dock, Canon's Marsh, 1826. (T. Rowbotham BMG M2924)

there was less traffic making its way up the Avon as larger and larger ships came into more general use around the world. In common with other, larger and more successful ports such as Liverpool and London, the commercial role of the Floating Harbour was finished off by the global switch-over to containerisation in the early 1970s. This was a tide of change that the port authorities were powerless to withstand, and in 1969 the City Council promoted legislation to end navigation rights within the harbour. In the event these rights were not removed but nevertheless the attempt signalled the end of the Floating Harbour as a commercial port.

The closure of the docks was followed by a period of uncertainty and a number of false starts in terms of regeneration, not helped by the years of economic recession in the early 1980s and again in the early '90s. Several housing schemes were built at different places around the harbour in the 1980s, including the site of the filled-in Champion's Dock at Rownham, but much dereliction remained, along the Redcliffe side of the water, opposite Welsh Back and at Canon's Marsh, where the goods yard closed down in 1965. Some would see the construction of the Lloyd's Bank head offices at Canon's Marsh in 1990 as marking a turning point in the regeneration.

In addition to telling the story chronologically we want to pursue a number of themes that run through the history of the Floating Harbour. These are all inter-related but for ease of discussion we can separate them out. First is the issue of governance, or who decides what gets done, when and by whom. A major infrastructural facility like the Floating Harbour requires large amounts of capital investment not just to build it in the first place but to maintain and develop it over a long period of time. Ways have to be found, therefore, of raising the capital, and then generating sufficient income to service the debt. Decisions about how to keep the port up to date with changes in the demands of ship owners were often highly charged political matters. From the outset the Floating Harbour was the responsibility of the Dock Company, a body specially set up to manage the project and to generate the income to service the debt. There was so much

criticism of the Dock Company that eventually the City Council took over in 1848, and has remained in charge ever since.

A second theme concerns the physical development of the port infrastructure – the provision of improved and larger locks, the building of more wharves to increase the capacity of the harbour, the construction of quayside sheds to store goods in transit, the provision of powered cranes and the development of railway connections to the quays. These were the responsibility of the port authorities, and over time the Floating Harbour was transformed by incremental investment, so that by the time of its closure as a commercial port it was more extensive and had more handling capacity than at any previous date.

A third theme is economic: to develop the infrastructure the authorities needed to generate income, the main source of which was the charges made to ship owners and others using the harbour. But of course, attracting ships to the port required that the infrastructure was up to date, and the charges were competitive. It is important to remember here that ports are essentially gateways, not destinations in themselves, and shippers have choices about which gateway to use for moving their goods around. The economics of the Floating Harbour were affected by several factors, including, initially, the debt burden arising from the construction work of 1804-09 which contributed to high port dues. The nature of the hinterland was another factor; compared with Liverpool, with its proximity to the burgeoning cotton industry of Lancashire, the Bristol region did not generate the same levels of port-related economic activity. Later the economic attractions of the port were constrained by the fact that ships of more than 330 feet in length simply could not negotiate the bends on the river.

Fourth, the impact of technological change; ports in general face the problem of coping with innovations over which they have little or no control: ships of increasing dimensions, driven by steam, and changes to increase the efficiency of cargo handling and storage methods. Technological innovation and economics work together

The Floating Harbour in 2007, showing the regeneration of Canon's Marsh. (PM slide 43)

in complex ways, and it is not a simple case of technology driving the pace of change. For example, Bristol was at the forefront of innovation in steamship design and construction in the late 1830s and early 1840s – Brunel's ships, the *Great Western* (1837) and the *Great Britain* (1843), were both the largest ships in the world when they were built – but smaller, wooden sailing ships went on bringing cargoes into Bristol for many years. The rate of take-up of technological innovation is determined by economics, and where it remained profitable to use established technologies they survived. Steam tended to be more successful on shorter routes in the early days, but after about 1865 improvements in the efficiency of steam engines meant that it was possible to obtain much more power from less coal. Longer routes became economically viable and from that point onwards the ascendancy of steam power was assured. This had implications for ports in general and in the Floating Harbour there was considerable infrastructural development after 1870, responding to the greater influx of larger steam powered vessels.

A final theme concerns the changing nature of the cargoes coming and going through the harbour. The success of a port can be influenced by possession of specialised equipment for handling or storing particular sorts of cargo, but equally, general-purpose mixed cargo ports were more successful than those that specialised in one type of commodity, such as coal. Bristol was always a mixed port, but it also mainly handled imports. The nature of cargoes influences both the economic success of a port and its physical appearance. Bristol had been very successful in the eighteenth century because of its strength in the West Indian trade based on importing mainly sugar. When that trade declined after 1800 the port suffered until new cargoes were found. From the middle of the century increasing amounts of grain were brought in, and some very large buildings were put up as a result, including the Corporation Granary at Wapping and Baker's mills at Redcliffe Back. Later, in the early decades of the twentieth century there was an increase in the volume of tobacco being imported to the Floating Harbour, giving rise to a series of huge bonded warehouses, three of which still dominate the entrance to the harbour from Cumberland Basin. Another staple commodity was timber, which was imported in quantity and stored in distinctive open-sided sheds, notably at Baltic Wharf.

In the chapters that follow we explore the first 200 years of the Floating Harbour through the four transformations and themes discussed here. We raise questions about how and why the harbour developed in the way that it did over that long period of time. We also introduce some of the key people who have influenced the course of events: Rev. William Milton, who in 1791 came up with the plan that was the basis of the scheme eventually implemented; William Jessop, who had overall responsibility for the work of 1804-09; I K Brunel, who had a long relationship with the harbour as consultant to the Dock Company; William Proctor Baker, influential member of the Docks Committee in the late nineteenth century; Thomas Howard and John Girdlestone, docks engineers; Dennis Ross Johnson and Alderman Henry Twiggs, whose leadership in the 1920s saw the city's policy change to favour development at Avonmouth.

1. Latimer, 1903, Buchanan and Cossons, 1969, MacInnes, 1968, Morgan, 1993, 1996
2. Reid and Hicks, 1877, Wells, 1909, Neale 1968, 1970 and 1976, Large 1984, Shipsides and Wall 1981, 1992, Lord and Southam, 1983
3. Buchanan, 2002, Kelly and Kelly, 2006
4. Bird, 1963 and Jackson, 1983

2 Planning and Building the Floating Harbour

Some accounts suggest that the construction of the Floating Harbour was prompted by Bristol's declining status and standing relative to other port cities, notably Liverpool. It can be portrayed as an attempt to catch up with the city's northern rival, but a more accurate interpretation is that it was a product of economic success and prosperity; it was growing numbers of ships using the harbour in the 1750s that led to complaints about overcrowding and the attendant dangers of congestion. Only a rich and prosperous city could contemplate port improvement of this nature and scale. The possibility of improving the port by keeping ships afloat at the quays as a way of dealing with congestion was under discussion before Liverpool overtook Bristol in the value of its port trade. However, Liverpool had already opened the world's first commercial wet dock, in 1715, and added more docks in 1788 and 1796. Hull opened the first large dock, in 1778, and London, too, was building its first docks, the West India Dock, opened in 1802.[1] By the 1790s dock building had become fashionable.

Bristol in the Eighteenth Century

Since the medieval period Bristol had been one of the largest towns in England, and a major port. In the early decades of the eighteenth century Bristol was the second port of the nation after London.[2] Much has been written about the growth of the wealth of the city's merchants and colonial estate owners on the back of the notorious 'triangular trade' in which Bristol ships were responsible for transporting almost half a million enslaved Africans across the Atlantic to the Caribbean and the mainland colonies of North America.[3] It is important to be clear that although wealth generated *from* the slave trade undoubtedly contributed to the construction of the Floating Harbour, it was not built *for* ships engaged in that trade. The new harbour was not completed until after the abolition of the slave trade in 1807, and in any case Bristol merchants had already withdrawn from the trade. But it is true that many of the ships that later used the new facility were bringing in cargoes of sugar and tobacco produced by slave labour.

In 1668 Samuel Pepys[4] described Bristol as 'in every respect another London', and called the quay 'a most large and noble place'. But it is the eighteenth century that is often seen as Bristol's 'golden age', when the city was the commercial capital and metropolis of the west.[5] The population had grown from about 20,000 in 1700 to more than 60,000 by the time of the first census in 1801, and as a result new suburbs such as Clifton, Kingsdown and St Paul's had grown up beyond the tight confines of the ancient city. The prosperous merchant class moved out to these more salubrious neighbourhoods, building elegant squares and fine mansions. In addition to the new suburbs there was a considerable amount of rebuilding in the central area. The old Bristol Bridge, with houses and shops in the style of London Bridge, was rebuilt in the 1780s (London Bridge lost its shops and houses in the 1750s). Among the more prominent new buildings of the eighteenth century were the Royal Infirmary, the Exchange, the Theatre Royal, the Assembly Rooms and the Free Library, plus a number of churches – all indicators of Bristol's claim to be a thoroughly modern and progressive city. The Floating Harbour needs to be seen in this context of rapidly changing ideas about what constituted a modern city. There were certain sorts of buildings that were necessary for a city to establish a claim to be of the first rank, and arguably a harbour in which ships remained afloat at all times was becoming a necessity for port cities. It was a sign of progress and sophistication, demonstrating a decisive break with the primitive tidal port.

There was a certain amount of industrial expansion in Bristol, notably in sugar refining, brass and glass manufacturing. Some of this was concerned with processing raw materials imported from the Americas but there was also manufacturing of items such as steam

View of the Avon looking towards St Mary Redcliffe from Sea Banks
(Canon's Marsh), 1785. (N. Pocock BMG M64675)

engines that were exported to the colonies. However, the regional hinterland did not, or could not, match the growth achieved in the textile areas of Lancashire and the West Riding. By 1801 Bristol had been overtaken by the rapidly growing manufacturing centres of Birmingham and Manchester, and by its great port rival, Liverpool.[6] One view is that the trade of the port of Bristol had become dangerously specialised and over-reliant on imports from the West Indies.[7] Sugar refining and other activities associated with the West Indies trade provided plenty of work and wealth, although the local economy was adversely affected in the aftermath of American independence. Bristol was declining relative to other ports and manufacturing centres, but its merchant class remained rich and prosperous, and it is important to understand that the general trend in economic activity indicated growth in absolute terms. Some historians have been inclined to interpret Bristol's relative decline as a reflection of the complacency of its wealthy elite, easily outpaced by newer rivals possessed of greater entrepreneurial drive. 'There is, however, no consensus over the extent of the decline, its timing or its causes'.[8]

There is agreement in the literature that failure to improve the port was a factor in Bristol's relative decline. But before looking in detail at the prolonged wrangle over this issue we need to consider how the city and the port were run in the second half of the eighteenth century. Municipal government was the responsibility of the Corporation, which took its authority from royal charters dating back to 1373 when Bristol became the first place to be given the title of 'city and county'. The area covered by the Corporation's writ was very small, embracing no more than the modern city centre. However, the importance of the port was reflected in the fact that the Corporation had rights on the Avon as far up stream as Hanham and downstream right out into the Bristol Channel. The Corporation consisted of the mayor, 12 aldermen and 30 councillors; there were no elections, vacancies being filled by co-option, and members generally served for life.[9] The Corporation was, therefore, not remotely democratic. Rather, it was a power base for the economic and social elite of the city, essentially merchants and manufacturers. It was a closed and rather secretive organisation, which was jealous of its rights and privileges, but reluctant to acknowledge responsibilities to provide public services beyond the administration of justice.

The Corporation owned significant amounts of property, including the quays which provided a source of income, for every ship entering the port had to pay a series of charges, plus any dues on cargo. In addition to Town Dues there was a levy known as the Mayor's Dues, the proceeds of which were used to help the mayor cover the costs of his office, which required a lot of entertaining, eating and drinking. The port was, then, a source of income for non-port related expenditure. In fact the Corporation had leased the quays to the Society of Merchant Venturers in the sixteenth century and it was this organisation that remained responsible for maintaining and improving the quays and the river. To raise the funds for these responsibilities the Society levied cranage, wharfage, plankage, anchorage and moorage dues on ships using the port. The SMV was the body that represented

The south end of Prince Street, 1826. (T. Rowbotham BMG M2928)

The view downstream from the Stone Bridge at the Quay Head, 1826. (T. Rowbotham BMG M2922)

the interests of the merchants and as such it was capable of exerting considerable influence within the city. Traditionally there was a good deal of overlapping membership between the Corporation and the Society, and fathers would nominate their sons, creating a clear tendency towards oligarchy in the management of municipal affairs, including the port.

In 1732 Alexander Pope memorably described the port of Bristol:

…in the middle of the street, as far as you can see, hundreds of ships, their masts as thick as they can stand by one another, which is the oddest and most surprising sight imaginable. This street is fuller of them than the Thames from London Bridge to Deptford, and at certain times only, as the water rises to carry them out; so that, at other times, a long street, full of ships in the middle and houses on both sides, looks like a dream.[10]

At the time of Pope's visit the quay wall was still incomplete but much of the riverbank from the quayhead on the Frome round to Bristol Bridge on the Avon had been made up. By the end of the century the job was done, turning Bristol into

…one of the finest mercantile havens in Europe; it is upwards of a mile in extent, reaching from St Giles' Bridge to Bristol Bridge, and is all the way embanked by a firm wall coped with large hewn stone, from which to the front buildings is such a considerable breadth, without interruption, as to make it one continued wharf. It goes under several distinct names, that part of it from Bristol Bridge to the turn of the river opposite Redcliffe Parade, is called the Back; and from hence following the course of the river downwards, is called the Grove; here is a dock [the Mud Dock] dug out from the river, which will contain ten large ships; further on is also another similar dock; on the west side of this last is a building, erected on fourteen pillars of cast iron, called the Great Crane, used for loading

and unloading ships lying at this dock; it is a curious piece of mechanism, constructed by the ingenious Mr Padmore…; from hence to the mouth of the Froom, is called the Gibb. All these parts of the Quay are formed on the banks of the main river, called the Avon.

This is a quote from a guide written in 1793. It continues in reference to the eastern side of the Frome, described by Wells[11] as 'the quay proper':

Here the greater number of shipping lie, and make a noble appearance; the vast quantities of different merchandise daily seen on the wharfs, are a convincing proof of the very great trade carried out in the port of Bristol. There are many cranes erected in proper places…; and opposite to the different parts of the quay are several yards for building and repairing ships… From St Augustine's Back over the Froom, is a Drawbridge much admired for the simplicity of its construction; it requires only one person on each side of the river to raise it for the Severn trows and other vessels to pass through during the time of the tides; these trows are generally stationed between this and another bridge about two hundred yards higher up, called St Giles' Bridge, which terminates the Quay on one end, as does Bristol Bridge on the other.

Impressive as it clearly was to all who saw it, by the middle of the eighteenth century the harbour was in need of improvement: it was overcrowded, its efficiency was greatly reduced by the grounding of ships for hours every day, it was a fire hazard and it was becoming a visual and aesthetic embarrassment to a city with pretensions to grandeur. Keeping ships permanently afloat within the port was seen as the solution to all of these problems. As a way of dealing with overcrowding it was better than, and an alternative to, simply building more quays, for it allowed the existing quays to be used more efficiently.

The Struggle for Harbour Improvement

By the 1720s ships of more than 150 'tons burden' were struggling to get up the Avon[12] but in that decade and again in the 1740s work was carried out to improve the river and to make it easier for larger ships to reach Bristol.[13] Attention then turned to the question of the harbour itself. The story of the debate that preceded the construction of the Floating Harbour divides into three quite distinct phases: 1755-67, 1786-93 and 1801-04. It is not necessary to describe each of the proposals – there were at least 18[14] – but it is interesting to note how plans developed over time, and how estimated costs rose. The city authorities consulted the leading civil engineers of the day, but there were also submissions from others less obviously qualified to comment on challenging technical problems. It was one of these amateur engineers, the Rev William Milton, vicar of Temple (a riverside parish in the old city), who came up with the idea of a new course for the river Avon and a 'feeder canal' to keep the harbour supplied with fresh water.

The problem was simply stated: in order to keep ships afloat at the quayside when the tide retreated it was necessary to construct a dam to hold back the water. But of course ships had to get in and out, and if access was to be available for more than the hour or two either side of high tide then a system of locks was required. If the principles were easily set out the question of where to build the dam and entrance facilities caused much debate. The dam needed to be constructed at a suitable location, preferably at a point far enough downstream for ships to be able to approach even on neap tides. This is an important point, because it reminds us that the location of the dam and entrance locks was based on the efficiency with which ships could be brought up to the existing quays, and not on any ambition to increase the extent of those quays. The subsequent expansion of the port to take advantage of the large area of non-tidal river bank was opportunistic and unforeseen by the builders of the Floating Harbour. A second issue to be resolved was the need to find a way to retain the power of the tides in the river (especially important in the days of sail), while

Shipbuilding at Eastern Wapping Dock (later Bathurst Wharf), 1826. (T. Rowbotham BMG M2951)

eliminating their effect within the harbour.

According to Latimer's account the Corporation was not generally disposed to support modernisation and it was the Society of Merchant Venturers that made most of the running.[15] McGrath, however, takes a rather different view, suggesting that the Society was not necessarily keen on expensive improvements, and it would be wrong to see the prolonged debate over the harbour as simply a power struggle between these two bodies.[16] Indeed McGrath also raises the possibility that the Society and the Corporation were combining to scupper improvement proposals in the 1760s by agreeing a new wharfage lease in 1764, well before the existing lease ran out.[17] Looking back from the twenty-first century modernisation was inevitable. We might also ask why the debate focused on improving the city centre harbour when the future lay at the mouth of the river. We need to look at the problem as it appeared to people at the time, not as it appears to us. Then there was no question of moving the port to Avonmouth, for two very good reasons: a river-mouth port would not solve the problem, because in those days, before the arrival of the railways, the river remained the best way to transport cargoes over long distances. Deep-draughted ships were already routinely anchored in the deep water at Hung Road, near the mouth of the river, from where their cargoes were carried into Bristol by barges, but merchants preferred not to do this, as it increased opportunities for pilferage and reduced prices.[18] Second, there was a strong preference among merchants and others whose businesses depended on the port for remaining where they were, all located close to each other in the city centre. The dense social network of inter-connected businesses was threatened by any proposal to relocate the port's centre of gravity.[19] Champion's dock, started in 1762 at Rownham (not much more than a mile from Broad Quay), was believed to have been commercially unsuccessful because it was too far from the centre, so obviously new development seven miles further away was unwelcome. Thus modernising the harbour was not just a complex technical problem. It was also overlain by social, economic and political considerations.

Not everyone was ready to accept that the existing harbour needed improvement, especially if it would cost them money without any direct benefit. Docks were a new idea in the middle of the eighteenth century, and by no means certain to become established as the norm. 'The modern assumption that docks are an indispensable part of ports cannot be applied in any sensible fashion to the eighteenth century.'[20] The costs of improvement were certain to be high, but the returns were not guaranteed, especially once it became clear that Bristol was losing ground to other ports. Here the proposers and objectors both used the relative decline of Bristol to support their case: the modernisers argued that it was necessary to restore Bristol's position, while those opposed argued that decline meant that improvement was neither necessary nor justifiable. There were also objections based on concerns about problems of floods coming down the river, and of the dangers of silt and sewage building up within the harbour. The danger of ice forming in a more or less stagnant harbour was another

potential problem. Then there were vested interests to be considered, especially water mills at various points on both the Avon and the Frome that would lose their head of water if the harbour was kept at high tide level. Owners of dry docks within the harbour complained about the difficulties they would face.

It was in 1755 that the Corporation received a report on congestion in the port, but not until three years later was the Town Clerk instructed to advertise for proposals for the construction of a convenient wet dock.[21] The Corporation was not keen on expensive and extensive work, and opted for a very short-term solution by agreeing a new lease with the SMV, extending the Society's tenure on the quays in return for an undertaking to build more quay space. Then in 1764 a meeting of merchants resolved to raise up to £30,000 to keep ships afloat at the quayside. John Smeaton, the noted civil engineer and canal builder, was commissioned to produce a plan, which he submitted in January 1765. He suggested a dam across the Frome where it joins the Avon, and an entrance basin and locks constructed on Canon's Marsh. This would have kept the water at high tide level on the

Calcraft Lock (later Totterdown Lock), 1821. (H. O'Neill BMG M3383)

Entrance to Bathurst basin from the New Cut, 1822. (H. O'Neill BMG M3384)

Frome branch but the whole of the Avon would have remained tidal. The following year William Champion, a local entrepreneur who had recently constructed a wet dock at Rownham, proposed to dam the Avon just below his dock and to construct an entrance basin and locks. Champion's scheme would have kept the water in the same parts of the rivers now covered by the Floating Harbour, but there were obvious questions about how the proposed structures would cope with the highest tides and flood waters coming down the two rivers. These questions were important, not least because the very highest tides were prone to cause flooding in the city, and any harbour improvement scheme needed to act as a flood protection measure as well. This was an era of rapid advance in civil engineering skills, but it is unlikely that anyone had a clear understanding of the true consequences of interfering with the natural flows of water in such a remarkably tidal river system as the Avon and Frome.[22]

In such circumstances it is easier to do nothing, and for another 20 years there was no further action. Then in 1786 the SMV invited Smeaton to recommend an engineer. He nominated two, Joseph Nickalls and William Jessop, who came up with radically different proposals. Nickalls, then president of the Society of Civil Engineers,[23] was the first to suggest a dam well below Bristol, at a place called Black Rock, on the grounds that it was simple, cheap and, above all, the only way (in his opinion) to ensure that large vessels would be able to approach the harbour. Jessop, who went on to build the Floating Harbour, had learned his trade under Smeaton. He was a successful consulting engineer on harbour projects who built docks at Dublin in the 1790s and the West India Dock in London in 1800.[24] He produced a scheme not unlike that of Champion, two decades before, with a dam on the Avon at Vauxhall Point and an entrance basin where Cumberland Basin was eventually built. Smeaton reviewed the plans of Nickalls and Jessop, and came up with another one of his own, similar to Jessop's, and estimated to cost £74,000.

By this stage the idea of an entrance basin appeared as a feature of most proposals. It would be necessary to have locks to allow ships in and out of the harbour, but the entrance basin was an additional device that made it possible to move larger numbers of ships more efficiently. While the tide was low the basin could be stocked with ships waiting to go down river. At high tide all the gates on the entrance locks could be opened, both to admit ships that had come up on the tide and to allow the departure of ships waiting in the basin. This was much more efficient than locking ships out one at a time. As the tide fell the outer gates could be closed and water from the harbour let into the basin to lift the level so that ships could enter the harbour proper.

In 1791 the Society of Merchant Venturers proposed to the Corporation that they should establish a joint committee in order to make progress with harbour improvement, and the Corporation 'showed a temporary inclination to abandon the apathetic policy that had been so long pursued'.[25] The joint committee met 14 times between 6 January 1792 and 9 September 1793.[26] One of the first proposals they considered was submitted by Rev. William Milton. This was ambitious, and expensive (estimated at £159,000), twice as costly as any scheme so far put forward. It required the expensive excavation of a new course for the Avon between Rownham and Temple Meads, and the making of a canal from Netham to Temple Meads. The great advantage offered by Milton was that he showed how to deal with the problem of the tides and river floods by means of a bypass. He maintained the beneficial effects of the tides, allowing smaller boats to drift on the rising tide all the way up to Temple Meads before entering the harbour, thereby saving considerable manual labour and time in hauling them by hand. Equally, the tidal bypass preserved a current flowing past the harbour, thereby helping to carry ships to and from the entrance. In the days before steam power enabled ships to go where they liked whenever they liked, this was a vital consideration. Despite this, Milton's plan was rejected as too expensive and not sufficiently advantageous.

In December 1792 the committee discussed an independent proposal for a public meeting to open a subscription for turning Canon's Marsh into a floating dock. This prompted the committee to say that the Society and the Corporation were agreed that any scheme should be carried out for the public good and not for private gain. The committee recommended the Corporation and the Society 'to oppose any scheme which has private interest for its objective'.27 With the benefit of hindsight this is a very interesting statement, given that the Floating Harbour was taken into municipal ownership in 1848 and that most other ports were managed by not-for-profit trusts. However, in the context of 1792 it was probably a coded way of saying that only schemes approved by the Corporation and the Society would be acceptable.

By 1793 some momentum was at last building up and it was agreed that a Bill should be prepared seeking powers to improve the harbour. A parliamentary Bill was necessary for two reasons: to establish the authority necessary to acquire the land for the new course of the river,

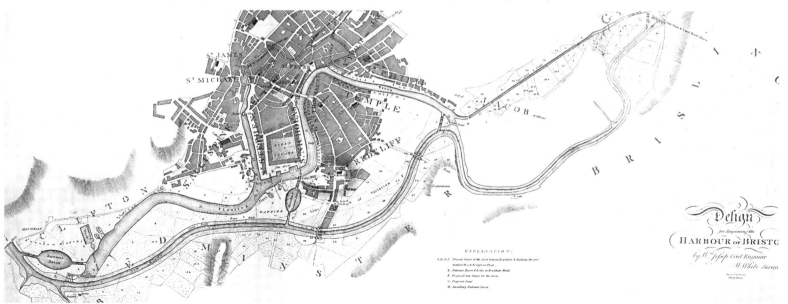

Jessop's Plan for the Floating Harbour, 1802. (D 9815/6)

Cumberland Basin and the New Cut from Rownham, 1825, showing Jessop's two entrance locks and the single junction lock into the Harbour. (S. Jackson BMG M970)

and to provide powers to establish a joint stock company to raise the large amounts of capital. Unfortunately, Britain went to war with France, trade fell away and no further action was taken until 1800. In July 1800 the SMV sought to stimulate action, but the Corporation continued to drag its feet.[28] Several schemes were considered between 1800 and 1802, including three from William Jessop in 1802 alone. In February 1802 Jessop was still proposing a limited scheme that would have left the Grove and the upstream arm of the Avon tidal, but by August he had made what proved to be the crucial change, extending the new cut for the Avon as far as Totterdown, and introducing a feeder canal between Netham and Temple Meads. This important and expensive change was, apparently, made in response to a suggestion to extend the new cut to Totterdown; the minutes of 2 August 1802[29] do not record whose suggestion it was but the committee asked William White to conduct the necessary survey and called Jessop to Bristol for two or three days to consider the evidence.

By this stage Jessop was probably ready to agree to more or less anything that would mean the project would be approved, for less than a fortnight later he explained his new plan to the committee, complete with a detailed estimate of costs.[30] Jessop's new plan, further revised in December 1802, bore a striking resemblance to the Milton proposal of 1791, albeit enhanced by a large entrance basin at Rownham and a new idea, not previously considered, for an additional entry basin for smaller vessels at Trim Mills (which became Bathurst Basin). However, Milton, the amateur, was not formally acknowledged as the originator of the solution and he later waged a long campaign for recognition, which culminated in his being awarded 'a piece of plate, not exceeding the value of one hundred guineas' by the Dock Company in 1803.[31] It seems unlikely that Jessop ever attempted to claim the credit for Milton's breakthrough; his biographers present him as a man of integrity, at the height of his powers as 'the greatest harbour engineer of his day'.[32]

In view of problems that were to occur later it is interesting to note that both sewage and silt were much discussed during the latter stages of the planning process. Jessop himself was dismissive of claims that sewage would be a problem, but nevertheless sought to reassure critics that he had made provision for intercepting most of the sewage discharged into the harbour.[33] On the question of silt and rubbish thrown into the harbour, the joint committee recorded

> *That two culverts of sufficient dimensions may if thought necessary be made through the lower part of the Dam at Rownham which may be drawn in times of Freshes [flood water coming down the river] and a very considerable under draught of Water procured by which means every advantage proposed by the Ground Sluices of the plan of 1792 will be obtained.*[34]

The total estimated cost was now put at £212,000, not including the cost of the land needed for the new cut, the entrance basins and the feeder canal.[35] The agreed plan was a very long way from Smeaton's first and apparently unaffordable £25,000 scheme in 1765. Naturally those opposed to change were not prepared to let this go without further argument, but this time their objections were easily overcome. After nearly half a century of 'caution, hesitancy and delay'[36] Bristol was on the brink of the most significant capital investment project ever undertaken in the city up to that time. By the end of 1802 there was not only an agreed plan of improvement works but also a decision had been made as to how the project would be paid for and managed. In March 1802 the joint committee proposed the formation of a board of directors comprised of the mayor and eight councillors, the master of the SMV and eight other members nominated by the Society, and nine shareholders. At that stage there was no plan to create a legally independent company, as is made clear by the detailed record in the minutes of decisions about payments of dividends and interest, and 'the principal to remain vested in the Corporation and the Society of Merchants for the general purposes of the port...'.[37] It was also decided in March 1802 to recommend that the Corporation and the Society should guarantee interest on the £50,000 mortgage, and that there should be a rate of 6d in the pound – generating £2,463 annually – on property in the city (not, at that time including suburbs such as Clifton where many of the merchants lived).

It was later decided to create the Dock Company as a separate legal entity, with a board of directors drawn from the Corporation, the Society and investors at large, in the same proportions as agreed in March 1802. This arrangement meant that the Dock Company was closely controlled by the traditional power élite, but neither the Corporation nor the SMV would carry any corporate financial or legal responsibility for its decisions and actions. It has been described as an 'early masterpiece of legal and financial manipulation'[38] and was to give rise to a great deal of ill-feeling over the next 45 years. The money, up to £300,000 (including the cost of land), was to be raised by a combination of share capital (£250,000) and loans (£50,000), with interest to be paid at 4 per cent for the first six years and 8 per cent thereafter.[39] Those who subscribed towards the share capital in-

cluded many leading merchants and other members of the business community in Bristol.[40]

During the summer of 1802 solicitors were instructed to draw up a Bill 'for improving and rendering more Commodious the Port and Harbour of Bristol'. This became the Bristol Dock Act, 1803. The Bill as initially drafted proposed that the Corporation and the SMV should guarantee the interest on the loans, but they refused and the clause was dropped. It was proposed that the main source of income for servicing the debt should come from charges on shipping. Not only did the Corporation and SMV refuse to carry any liability, they also insisted on continuing to collect their various dues from users of the port. Moreover, the 1803 Act provided for the assets of the Dock Company to revert to the Corporation once it had discharged its financial obligations incurred to build the Floating Harbour. The opposition carried on pressing their case throughout the construction process,[41] and the course of events gave them much to complain about.

Building the Floating Harbour

The two best accounts of the construction process itself are provided by Buchanan[42] and Hadfield and Skempton.[43] Buchanan[44] records that the first meeting of the Dock Company directors was in September 1803, just four months after the resumption of war with France – not propitious circumstances in which to begin a major undertaking. Work began with the excavation of the trench that would become the new course of the river Avon (the New Cut). Little is known about how the task was organised and carried out but the first contract was let to Thomas Thatcher and James Sharp, both described as canal cutters. Their task was to dig out about 750 yards to a specified depth, starting on 1 May 1804 in a field belonging to Sir Hugh Smyth just to the west of Dean Lane, Southville.[45] After so long in the planning the project was set off at 5 am when George Webb Hall, clerk to the Dock Company, ceremonially dug out the first spadeful of soil. The contrac-

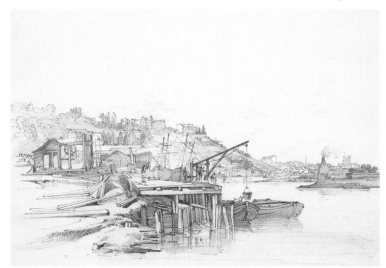

Drawn by Hugh O'Neill about 1805, this may show work on Cumberland Basin and as such is one of only two known images of the construction of the Floating Harbour. (H. O'Neill BMG M3368)

tors were given detailed instructions as to where they were to spread the material dug out from the trench. Just why the decision was made to start half way along the course of the new cut is not known. But what is known is that Thatcher and Sharp were required to complete their work by 1 October, and that they were then followed by different contractors, John Hodge, Robert Langman and William Dutton, also canal cutters, whose task was to dig out the stone from the bottom of the trench created by Thatcher and Sharp. They were to complete the job by 1 March 1806.[46]

J P Malcolm left the only description of how rock was blasted with explosives and then removed from the site:

The shock had not only rifted the rock immediately surrounding the powder, but huge fragments were removed from their beds and where wedges were driven into them, and they are thus reduced small enough to be raised by cranes by four men into carts which were conveyed up the bank by operation of steam engines erected on the verge of the canal. The engines turned several wheels with strong chains round them, which by their revolutions lowered, emptied and raised the filled carts attached to the chains.[47]

Meanwhile, Thatcher and Sharp were commissioned to dig out the entrance basin and lock pit at Rownham (Cumberland Basin) between December 1804 and September 1805.[48] However, Thatcher and Sharp seem to have dissolved their partnership for later contracts were let to Thatcher alone and then to Thatcher and Richards, who were awarded the contract to build the Cumberland Basin entrance locks in November 1805.[49]

These contractors were working under the day-to-day supervision of William Jessop's son, Josias, who was paid £500 per year as deputy engineer and superintendent of works – or project manager in today's jargon. It was clearly a very large and challenging project, employing around 1,000 men. Most of the work must have been done by

Harford's Bridge (later Bedminster Bridge) over the New Cut, 1821. (H. O'Neill BMG M2956)

hard manual labour, although several steam engines were purchased to pump water out of the workings. The Cumberland Basin was to cover six acres 'at least', and to have two entrance locks of different sizes and two junction locks communicating with the harbour; one of these was to connect through the Merchants' Dock (Champion's original wet dock). The river was to be blocked by an overfall dam, ie it was to be constructed so that excess water within the harbour would overflow into the tidal river. A key passage in the Act said that the dam should be 'provided with Culverts, Sluices and ground Hatches, for the purpose of scouring the Floating Harbour, and laying the same dry whenever necessary for the purpose of Repairs…'.[50] The problem of silting-up and the need to scour the harbour had been properly anticipated and provided for by Jessop.

The Act went on to specify further dams at Temple Meads (where there was to be an entrance lock for barges) and Engine Mills (Netham). There was also to be a second entrance basin at Trim Mills (Bathurst

Basin, named after Charles Bathurst, a Bristol MP during 1796-1811). The excavation of the New Cut, necessitated the construction of two iron bridges designed by Jessop (they were known as Hill's Bridge and Harford Bridge and stood on the sites of the modern Temple Meads and Bedminster bridges respectively). Finally the Act specified the construction of the Feeder Canal, the purpose of which was to maintain the supply of water and to ensure a current that would help to prevent silting-up.

In September 1805 the directors reported to shareholders that good progress was being made. But almost inevitably things began to go wrong. There were accidents, such as the collapse of the partially build bridge over the New Cut at Temple Meads, and delays due to unforeseen soil conditions. Very little is known about the labourers who toiled to build the Floating Harbour but from *Felix Farley's Bristol Journal*, 14 February 1807, comes a glimpse of their capacity to make their feelings known:

> *Last week a refractory disposition showed itself among the labourers, principally the diggers, on the New Cut, in this city; and on Friday a body of them refused to work. Their pretended grievance was, an undue exaction on the part of the contractor, respecting the hour of breakfast. Their example was followed by the whole line of diggers, about 400 in number, and threats were advanced of stoning all workmen of every denomination who persisted in working until their supposed grievance was redressed. In consequence of this, about 800 workmen suspended their labour, and as one motive of discontent is too frequently made subservient to another, the rioters required an advance of wages; but their demands in both cases were so unreasonable and ill-judged, that the contractor, much to his credit, persisted in refusing to comply with them; and the men, after losing three quarters of a day, returned to their labour.*

Jessop had intended to leave both the Cumberland and Bathurst Basins unlined, but in the event they had to be lined with masonry. This obviously added considerably to the expense, with the result that under a second Act, obtained in 1806, Cumberland Basin was reduced to four acres. The Act also permitted Jessop to modify the Rownham dam as a cost-saving measure. Jessop's plan of 1792 had shown a masonry dam penetrated by a series of six large openings with sluice gates, and four ground hatches, two at each end of the dam. This elaborate structure was designed to allow rapid lowering of the water level within the harbour, aiding the scouring process, and although Jessop's explanation of his 1803 plans is not specific on this matter it can be safely assumed that he was still thinking in the same terms. The new Act, however, permitted the building of a 'solid' dam with an overfall to one side, allowing excess water from the harbour to run out into the New Cut. Despite references to a solid dam the Act went on to specify the inclusion within the overfall of 'culverts, sluices and ground hatches for the purpose of scouring and emptying the harbour' in exactly the same words as in the Act of 1803. There was an important difference between the plan of 1792 and the scheme as built. Jessop's earlier idea had required the dam to handle the full flow of both the Avon and Frome whereas by the time the dam came to be built most of any flood water was safely carried away via the bypass. This may have convinced him that a solid dam and reduced overfall would suffice.

The Act also allowed the Company to raise additional capital to meet rising costs. This did not solve the difficulties and further legislation was prepared the following year, although the Bill was opposed by the Corporation and had to be withdrawn and re-presented in 1808. This new Act allowed the Company to raise further capital, and specified that the work must be completed by 1 May 1809. As with many big capital projects, modifications continued to be made as work progressed. Two notable changes under the 1808 Act were the omission, on grounds of economy, of one of the two junction locks between the harbour and the Cumberland Basin, and the granting of powers to construct two piers jutting out into the harbour at the site

Cumberland Basin locks under construction, about 1808. (G. Holmes BMG K2356)

of the modern Prince Street bridge. These piers would allow a swing bridge to be thrown across the harbour and also enable the harbour to be divided into two parts, by means of gates between the piers, to allow one half to be drained for maintenance purposes while ships remained afloat in the other half. In principle all ships were to be removed from the half to be drained and the work of the port could continue with less disruption.

Water was first let into the New Cut in January 1809[51] and the Floating Harbour was officially completed and opened on 1 May 1809, exactly five years after work began, and 54 years after the idea of a wet dock was first raised. The successful completion of the project was marked by an open-air dinner for 1,000 of the workers involved, in a field between the harbour and the New Cut. A number of participants became over-excited, and a considerable fracas, apparently involving rival groups of English and Irish labourers, occurred in Marsh Street and Prince Street. There were numerous arrests and personal injuries.[52] Little more is known about the men who actually built the Floating Harbour, but as Angus Buchanan[53] noted, there is no evidence to support the persistent local tradition that it was dug by French prisoners of war.

View across the New Cut to the Floating Harbour and the city beyond, 1827. (T. Rowbotham BMG M3413)

The final cost, almost double Jessop's estimate of 1802, was £594,000, equivalent to more than £34 million today. According to Wells[54] the basins at Trim Mills and Rownham were £100,000 over budget, and land purchase for the New Cut involved an unforeseen outlay of £66,000. Many critics have pointed to the damaging impact of the length of time taken to agree a plan, then to bring the project to fruition and the failure to curb costs, with the result that the Dock Company was saddled with a huge debt that it struggled to repay from income. On the other hand, delay and cost over-runs were normal in this sort of project, as Liverpool and Hull had recently demonstrated. And what was actually built in Bristol was technically a fine solution to a difficult set of engineering problems. The fact that modifications were later shown to be necessary, especially those associated with the increased size of ships, should not detract from the achievement of the Jessops and their backers, who could not be expected to foresee either the economic growth or the technological changes that lay ahead.

1. Jackson, 1983
2. Jackson, in Clark, 2000: 708
3. Dresser, 2007: 28
4. Pepys, 1906: 660
5. Minchinton, 1954 quoted in Williams, 1962, Minchinton, in McGrath, 1972
6 Langton, J 2000 p 473
7 MacInnes, 1968: 358
8. Morgan, 1996: 49
9. Bush, 1976: 18
10. *Letters to Martha Blount*, quoted in Williams, 1962
11. Wells, 1909: 31
12. Bird, 1963:187
13. Williams, 1962
14. ibid
15. Latimer, 1903
16. McGrath, 1975: 151
17. ibid: 153
18. McGrath, in Minchinton: 146
19. Jackson, 1983: 46
20. ibid: 47
21. Wells, 1909, 22
22. Williams, 1962: 164
23. Hadfield and Skempton, 1979: 224
24. ibid, 1979, Jackson, 1983, 53
25. Latimer, 1903: 213-4
26. BRO, SMV/7/1/4/7
27. BRO, SMV/7/1/4/7
28. McGrath, 1975: 307
29. BRO, SMV/7/1/4/7
30. reproduced in Buchanan, 1969
31. Williams, 1962: 179
32. Hadfield and Skempton, 1979: 257
33. BRO, SMV/7/1/4/7, letter dated 14 August 1802
34. minutes of 20 November 1802
35. Williams, 1962: 178, Buchanan, 1969: 189
36. Williams, 1962: 180
37. BRO, BCC, SMV/7/1/4/7
38. Neale, 1968: 3
39. Wells, 1909: 35-6
40. ibid: 42-5
41. Buchanan, 1969: 190n
42. Buchanan, 1969
43. ibid
44. ibid: 191
45. BRO, BCC/D/PBA/Corp/E/3/35a
46. BRO, BCC/D/PBA/Corp/E/3/35c
47. quoted in White, 2006, p13-14
48. BRO, BCC/D/PBA/Corp/E/3/35e(i)
49. Hadfield and Skempton, 1979: 236.
50. quoted by Buchanan, 1969: 190
51 Wells, 1909: 52
52. Reid and Hicks, 1878: 70, Wells, 1909: 53
53. Buchanan, 1969
54. Wells, 1909: 48

Completion of the Floating Harbour was a considerable achievement, giving Bristol 'the largest area of impounded water for shipping in the world' at that time.[1] After so much dithering and delay Bristol had a harbour capable of competing with its rivals, heralding the possibility of a return to its former position in the league table of British ports. Unfortunately, the story of what happened next is one of continued relative decline and failure to make the most of the potential embodied in the Floating Harbour. Existing accounts generally place the responsibility for this squarely on the shoulders of the Dock Company. However, the reality was more complicated, and more interesting.

The population of Bristol continued to grow strongly in the first four decades of the nineteenth century, from 60,000 in 1801 to 125,000 in 1841,[2] a sure sign that the city as a whole was still sufficiently prosperous to attract migration from the surrounding counties. By the 1830s the built-up area extended far beyond the boundaries of the ancient city, drawn up in 1373. The boundaries were therefore moved outwards under the provisions of the Municipal Corporations Act, 1835. The newly incorporated areas included the high-value neighbourhood of Clifton, part of Westbury and parts of Bedminster, St Pauls, St James and St Philip and Jacob.[3] The inclusion of Clifton was to have an important impact of the politics of the Floating Harbour later in the century. The 1835 Act abolished the old close Corporation, replacing it with a new town council which was elected by the ratepayers of the city. The Act did not introduce a full adult franchise but it was a step towards a more open and democratic system of local government, and as such can be seen as a pre-condition for reform of the governance of the Floating Harbour in the 1840s.

Some writers have referred to an urban renaissance in the 1830s, embracing vigorous commercial expansion,[4] and Buchanan[5] refers to a 'spirited commercial revival' in Bristol in the 1830s and '40s.

Although industries such as glass manufacturing and sugar refining declined, others, such as the Great Western Cotton factory (established in 1838) were growing. It was in the 1830s that Bristol businessmen began a new wave of ambitious capital projects, including the Clifton Suspension Bridge and the Great Western Railway. Against this background the continued paucity of investment in the harbour is thrown into starker relief.

For decades after 1809 the scene in much of the Floating Harbour remained charmingly rural, with natural river banks still in place and cattle continuing to graze in the fields on the Wapping side. But there was also substantial ship building at Wapping, notably Patterson's yard, where the *Great Western* was built in 1837, and Hilhouse's yard, opened in 1820, next to where the *Great Britain* now sits. There was also ship building and repairing on the other side of the harbour, for example, at Limekiln Dock opposite the bottom of Jacob's Well Road[6] and on a part of the Frome bank known as the Butts, as well as lower down, opposite the Bush Warehouse.[7]

The loading and unloading of ships continued to be concentrated around the ancient quays, as the relative decline of the port of Bristol continued. While Bristol baulked at further expenditure on port improvements after spending £600,000 on the Floating Harbour, Liverpool pressed ahead with investment in new docks in 1816, racking up an estimated total of £4 million between 1709 and 1836.[8] Whereas the volume of trade passing through Liverpool doubled between 1815 and 1830, and doubled again by 1845,[9] in Bristol overseas trade actually declined in absolute terms between 1791 and 1841, although coastal traffic tripled in the same period.[10] Overall tonnage of trade through Bristol rose by 122% between 1791 and 1841. Having done very well out of certain activities and practices in the eighteenth century Bristol merchants seemed to be reluctant to change with the times. It has been said that Bristol's trade had be-

In 1825, and for many more years, the Bedminster and Canon's Marsh banks of the Floating Harbour remained undeveloped. (S. Jackson BMG M979)

Port of Bristol Authority offices at Queen Square, built in 1886, pictured in 1937. (PBA 676)

come 'dangerously concentrated on the West Indies',[11] and that 'in the first half of the nineteenth century Bristol…fought and lost many battles in defence of the old order'.[12] From the point of view of Bristol merchants, it could be argued, the important measure was that their own wealth and that of Bristol was increasing; what was happening elsewhere was, in one sense, irrelevant. Against that, people were well aware of, and concerned about, the relative decline of Bristol, and it is clear that there was real rivalry and competition between ports, especially Bristol and Liverpool. The combination of a powerful but conservative elite and an expensive, debt-burdened, port was not a recipe for success in competition with ambitious rivals better placed to take advantage of the opportunities opening up in an increasingly dynamic economy.

The contrast between Bristol and Liverpool suggested a straightforward remedy. Liverpool had invested more heavily in develop-ing the port, but charged individual shippers less, and trade grew more strongly. Not surprisingly, the authorities in Bristol now faced demands for more investment and lower charges as a way of stimulating growth. Two points need to be made here: first, there is a chicken-and-egg problem in understanding the relationship between ports and their hinterlands. Does a cheap port encourage economic growth inland, or does a strong local economy generate the volumes of trade that justify low port charges? Like all such problems, this is not easy to resolve. Second, from the point of view of the Bristol Dock Company, it was asking a lot for them to invest yet more capital and to reduce charges with no guarantee that trade would increase.

This chapter looks at the governance of the Floating Harbour from 1809 to 1848, when the Dock Company was taken over by the Town Council. 'The record of [these] years is one of a fatuous policy, which, by her supineness, reduced Bristol from her proud position of the second seaport in the kingdom, drove trade away from her by exorbitant dues and suffered Liverpool and other ports to outbid her for the commerce of the world.'[13] Throughout this period there were complaints and recrimination about the cost of constructing the Floating Harbour, the resulting high dues levied by the Dock Company, and the Company's reluctance to try to increase trade by further port improvements and/or lower charges. 'There were many cases of great personal bitterness between citizens for a long time over these questions'.[14] It is hard to find anyone with anything positive to say about the Dock Company during this period, and neither the Corporation nor the Society of Merchants, standing behind the Dock Company, had much to be proud of in their attitude to the port.

The Dock Company

The Dock Company operated from modest offices in Broad Street, in the heart of the old city, close to the Council House and the Guildhall. In January 1847, shortly before its demise, the Company moved to 18 Queen Square (in 1886, after the takeover of the docks at Avonmouth

The New Cut and the New Gaol, seen from Harford's Bridge, 1821. (H. O'Neill BMG M3376)

and Portishead the Council bought numbers 19 and 20 Queen Square and erected new offices on the site[15]). The directors of the Company held regular weekly meetings, although the numbers attending were generally well below the 27 who were entitled to be there. The Company has been denounced as a piece of financial chicanery,[16] giving the Corporation and SMV power without financial responsibility, but there is no evidence that individual directors were personally corrupt. It can also be seen as an early example of local strategic partnership working. While it is easy to criticise the performance of the Company, if we look at the situation as it appeared to the people promoting the Floating Harbour in 1803 its creation seems sensible. What else could they have done? Liverpool had developed its docks in the eighteenth century through municipal initiative, and apparently there was never any doubt that the Corporation would take responsibility there.[17] Having said that, by the time Bristol was deciding how to proceed, the Liverpool docks committee was 'actively transforming itself into a semi-independent trust'.[18] In Bristol the Corporation had no tradition of investing in the port, quite the opposite in fact. The Corporation had a 300-year history of milking the port for revenue, leaving the Society of Merchants to build quay walls, provide cranes and improve the river. When Hull sought to build a dock in the 1770s the decision was made to opt for a private company, which was very successful at first but 'erstwhile supporters soon viewed Hull Dock Company as a recipe for disaster'.[19] The problem was that success led to demands for further dock building, but the company enjoyed monopoly rights and had no incentive to jeopardise its profits by new building, either by itself or anyone else. Elsewhere, the first wave of dock building in London coincided with the later stages of discussion about the Floating Harbour, and here too private enterprise took the lead.[20]

So there was a range of different approaches already in existence. Although there appears to be no evidence that decision makers in Bristol investigated or considered the strategies adopted elsewhere it is unlikely that they were unaware of them. Bristol devised its own solution, and it is arguable that the chosen model was perfectly

The Bush Warehouse, Narrow Quay, built by thriving engineers the Acraman family in the early 1830s, pictured in 1959. (PBA N2077)

reasonable, given what the people involved knew at the time. The problem came later, first because of escalating costs (which were probably uncontrollable given the nature of the project and the techniques available at the time), and then because of how the parties controlling the Company chose to react. Maybe the Company has been credited with greater independence than it actually possessed, and perhaps the finger of blame should point to the partners, the Corporation and the Society of Merchant Venturers.

The Dock Company was run by a board of directors consisting of equal numbers nominated by the Corporation, the Society of Merchants and other investors. Its powers and responsibilities were set out in the four Docks Acts of 1803-09. It was empowered to carry out the work necessary to construct the Floating Harbour, and to raise income to meet its liabilities, the main one being the servicing of the debt of more than £268,000 incurred in building the harbour.

The rest of the capital had been subscribed by shareholders, who had expectations of regular dividends (although none was paid until 1823).[21] The Act of 1803 included a long list of items on which dues were payable to the Company, and the same list in the Act of 1808 shows that in nearly every case the rate had been increased. The fact that the Company was forced to increase charges to meet its liabilities but could still not pay a dividend inevitably fuelled criticism of its stewardship. But it had no choice. In the accounts for the year to May 1812, for example, £20,008 was paid out in interest, but income from dues was only £15,231. In that year the Company also repaid £30,000 to Richard Hart Davis, a former treasurer, and one of the original backers of the Floating Harbour project.[22]

The Dock Company was also responsible for the cleanliness and depth of the water within the harbour, although it had very little spare cash for this purpose. The Company owned land adjacent to the entrance basins and the New Cut (some of this land was sold over the years) but it did not own any wharves or quays. Nor was it responsible for the maintenance or improvement of the quays, which remained the property of the Corporation, and were leased to the SMV. Given the importance attached to the issue of the high level of charges faced by shippers using the port, it needs to be emphasised that the Corporation and SMV continued to levy their various dues on top of what the Dock Company charged just to service the debt. If the Dock Company had no choice about the charges it levied in the port, was the same true of the Corporation and SMV? Could they have helped to improve Bristol's competitive position by reducing their demands? While individual merchants were undoubtedly wealthy, the Society's historian has emphasised its corporate poverty and dependence on the income from the wharfage lease.[23] The Corporation apparently took the view that its income was a form of private property to which it was perfectly entitled and which should not be questioned.[24] In 1820 Town dues amounted to £4,036, the second largest tranche of income for the Corporation, and so it is understandable that this would not be lightly given up.[25] In addition the Corporation claimed Mayor's

Celebration of Free Port Day, 13 November 1848. (S. Tovey BMG K106)

dues, water bailiff's fee, quay warden's fee and corn measurer's fee. The Society claimed dues for tonnage, wharfage, carriage, cannage, cranage and plankage.[26] Bringing a ship into Bristol must have been a highly bureaucratic experience.

It is true that the Dock Company has ever been the butt of criticism for its obduracy and unwillingness to act, while insisting on maximising its income. In MacInnes's view the Company was 'hidebound and unprogressive'.[27] But it is important to look at structural as well as behavioural factors in explaining decisions about the Floating Harbour in the years after its completion. The Company was in an unenviable position: as construction costs had soared they had looked for economies which contributed to problems requiring further substantial investment. This could not be afforded without further increases in charges, incurring yet more criticism and possibly driving away more trade. The Dock Company could be seen as trapped in an early version of Catch 22. The Company was a convenient scapegoat for problems not of its making and beyond its powers to resolve.[28] The fact that a majority of the directors were drawn from the Corporation and the SMV meant that it lacked both independence and the freedom to act in a truly businesslike fashion.

The Struggle Over Port Charges

According to Bush[29] the Corporation derived 11 per cent of its income from port dues in the period 1820-1835, and people using the port began to ask what they were getting from the Corporation in return; questions were also raised as to the legality of these dues, which were established by custom and practice rather than statute. It was in 1823 that the issue of port charges really came to a head, with the formation of a Chamber specifically to campaign for lower rates. The Chamber of Commerce was a body representing business interests in the city, a role traditionally associated with the SMV, but of course that organisation was responsible for appointing a third of the directors of the Dock Company and therefore not free to be as publicly

critical as it might otherwise have been. At the same time the debate was taken to the wider public by the editor of a local newspaper, *Felix Farley's Bristol Journal*.[30] Writing under the *nom de plume* of Cosmo he praised the Floating Harbour as a great achievement, and referred to the Dock Company as 'more sinned against than sinning' but called for lower port charges as a sure way of increasing overall trade and thus revenue. It was surely not coincidental that in August 1823 Dock Company shareholders received their first ever dividend (a mere 1 per cent, with 1.75 per cent the following year).[31] Increased public attention on the costs of the port, in a period when trade was static (revenue fell from a peak of £22,139 in 1819 to £17,707 in 1821 before recovering to £18, 494 in 1823),[32] put considerable pressure on the authorities. The campaign was led by the Chamber of Commerce, which first protested against the Corporation's levies. It was supported by the SMV, which, somewhat improbably, claimed that the 'languour and comparative decline of Bristol trade was mainly attributable to the Town and Mayor's dues.'[33] The Corporation responded by seeking to establish a statutory right to its dues, and an Act was passed in 1825.[34] This was a hollow victory for the right to challenge the legality of the dues remained unimpaired.[35] However, receipts from Town and Mayor's dues fell by more than half over the five years after 1825, so the campaigners had achieved something.

The real problem was the charges levied by the Dock Company (20 times the level of Town and Mayor's dues in 1837)[36] and the Chamber also made the case for an overall reduction in port charges by setting out a table comparing the cost of importing certain goods in Bristol, Liverpool, London and Hull. On a selection of 44 different import items Bristol was more than twice as expensive as London and Liverpool, and more than three times as expensive as Hull.[37] The same kind of comparison was published in 1833, again showing that on certain imported goods Bristol was very much more expensive than its rivals.[38] Port dues were criticised at other ports too, for ship owners wanted to load and unload vessels at uneconomically low rates; they wanted someone to provide expensive facilities at no cost to anyone.[39] In the summer of 1834 the Dock Company agreed to reduce its charges on a long list of items,[40] although this still left 'excessive charges on sugar, wine and tobacco'.[41]

In the run up to local government reform the government set up a royal commission, which sent out commissioners in 1833 to investigate the working of municipal corporations. The report on Bristol included the following telling summary:

> *The condition of the City of Bristol is indissolubly connected with the prosperity of its port; and it is notorious that the trade of Bristol has not kept pace with the increase of other ports, once its rivals. Far below her former station as the second port of the empire she now has to sustain a mortifying competition with second-rate ports in her own Channel. If it were not for its Irish trade and the West Indies monopoly, of which the circumstances still enable Bristol to retain its share, it is possible that there would soon be nothing in the Floating Harbour but a few coasters and fishing boats.*[42]

The situation was clearly serious, and in 1834 the Corporation appointed a committee to consider the question of Town Dues. When this committee reported the following March the Corporation agreed a list of reductions, some of them substantial.[43] Then in September 1835 it was resolved to abolish Town Dues on exports and to reduce dues generally, although the loss was less than £500 per year.[44] Within a year of coming into existence the new Town Council (which inherited the Corporation's right to nominate a third of the directors to the Dock Company) set up a permanent committee to investigate port charges. In 1837 a small reduction was obtained, with the SMV agreeing to give up its lease on the cranes and cranage dues.[45] But this was not enough to stem criticism of the state of the harbour and the adverse impact of tariffs on trade.

The Campaign for a 'Free Port'

A joint committee representing the council, the SMV, the Chamber of Commerce and the Great Western Steamship Company reported in July 1839 on ways to improve the harbour and reform its governance. Among its recommendations were suggestions for raising new share capital, abolishing the property rate contribution to port revenues and widening the representation of the board of directors of the Dock Company.[46] The Dock Company dismissed the recommendations, but eventually suggested that the advocates of reform should buy the Company's properties and put themselves in a position to see whether they could do a better job of running the port. Wells calls this the first practical suggestion for freeing the port,[47] but it is important to consider the shades of meaning that could attach to such an evocative and seductive term. Port facilities are inherently expensive to build and maintain, and have to be paid for by someone, so in that sense there is no such thing as a free port. The mid-nineteenth century was the era when free trade was being established, and in the 1840s the removal of the Corn Laws and the Navigation Acts certainly gave a great boost to trade and shipping. In this context a free port could imply a port where anyone could trade, without the sorts of restrictions on foreigners and privileges for locals that had traditionally applied in ports such as Bristol.

In fact, it seems that the advocates of a free port in Bristol had in mind a port free of 'all charges on goods and shipping inwards and outwards – except such trifling charges as may be necessary for the convenience of the port…'.[48] This left plenty of scope for debate about who was to pay, and how the money should be raised. In addition to the argument about comparative costs and rivalry between ports there was a further case for saying that the whole of the burden of port costs should not fall on shippers and traders: all sorts of people benefited from a thriving port to the extent that it directly generated profits and jobs for people supplying those who owned ships and traded in goods. Ships' chandlers, sack makers, barrel makers, sail makers

Hilhouse's new dock (later Albion Dockyard) seen from Mardyke, 1826. (T. Rowbotham BMG M2939)

and so on all benefited. Then there was another set of businesses that indirectly benefited from the general increase in the volume of money circulating in a thriving port. Needless to say, there was a strongly held counter-view, opposed to any attempt to relieve the burden on port users by spreading it across rate payers in the city as a whole, despite the evidence that economic prosperity increased property values at large. This view was loudly expressed by residents of Clifton in particular, who pointed out that they (being outside the city at the time) had had no part in the construction of the Floating Harbour.

The Dock Company directors nominated by the Town Council found themselves at loggerheads with the proprietary directors (nominated by the shareholders),[49] and soon people were reluctant to accept nomination. The Dock Company was blamed by almost everyone for the stagnant state of trade in the port, and there was widespread agreement that municipalisation was the only answer. The Council made its first offer to buy out the Dock Company in 1839, but was rebuffed. It tried again in 1845, and its offer was again deemed inadequate. It was then, in the autumn of 1846, that the Free Port Association was established, with Robert Bright as its president. The scion of a long-established family of Bristol merchants and ship owners with interests in the West Indies trade, Bright was a director of the Great Western Railway and the Great Western Cotton Factory, and was to play a leading role in the Free Port Association. The Association was supported, in those class-conscious days, by an Operatives Free Port Association representing the working class. As mentioned above, the idea of a truly free port was a fantasy, and it is perhaps better to see the campaign as primarily about ousting the reviled Dock Company and substituting a more acceptable form of ownership, which might be able to reduce but not eliminate port charges.

This time there was a build-up of momentum, backed by widespread popular support, and with a reformed Town Council now firmly in place it was possible at last to break the mould. The Association was well organised, amply funded and supported by the majority of local newspapers. A key part of the campaign was the publication of a series of *Free Port Tracts* addressing the main points for and against reform, but cultivating the idea that municipalisation was virtually inevitable.[50] In February 1847 the Council and the Association began to confer and in due course the Dock Company was persuaded to accept an offer. Shareholders and other investors were to become creditors of the Council, a rate of four pence in the pound would be levied on property in the city and port dues would be reduced by a specified amount (£9,400). Ratepayers in Clifton, who contributed nearly half the city's rates revenue, were inevitably unhappy. In February 1848 there was a public meeting in Broadmead Assembly Rooms said to be attended by 2-3,000 ratepayers to debate the issues.[51] In April a Bill to give effect to the proposed changes was considered by the Commons and received royal assent at the end of June. By municipalising its port Bristol was moving against the national trend. Liverpool, for example, handed over its port to a non-profit trust in 1858, whereas Bristol became the only important dock system run by a local authority.[52]

A new Docks Committee, chaired by a Redcliffe ship owner Councillor Richard Poole King, was appointed to take over the running of the port in August 1848. The Committee recommended reductions in dues on a wide range of items, saving port users about £12,000 a year. According to Wells[53] the burden on ships was reduced by about 50 per cent and on goods by about 20 per cent. Almost exactly forty years after the completion of the Floating Harbour the demise of the Dock Company and the substantial reductions in charges was a momentous change, celebrated with a public holiday on 13 November 1848. It is important to remember that the port was not free, and that the price of reduced charges was the imposition of an additional rates burden on the city as a whole. Some saw the municipal takeover as a triumph for the merchants at the expense of ratepayers in general. However, the Town and Mayor's dues carried on – in fact the income from these dues exceeded the rates contribution in 1849 and every year from 1860-1890.[54]

Trade passing through Bristol picked up immediately, and grew by two thirds in the next decade, compared with only one third in the two decades up to 1848.[55] This led a later commentator to claim that the Dock Company had been induced to sell out too soon.[56] The argument was that a number of external factors were working in favour of increased volumes of international trade: the repeal of both the Corn Laws and the Navigation Acts in the 1840s, together with the opening up of the North American prairies meant more grain was imported into Britain, and declining supplies of home-grown timber also boosted imports. Others have pointed in the same direction, noting that the middle decades of the nineteenth century were an era of rapid growth in the global economy, and that trade grew faster than industrial production.[57] It was the British economy that dominated world trade, especially in manufactured goods, and it was British ships that carried the majority of cargoes. So the criticism might be correct, or it could simply be that the municipalisation of the Floating Harbour came at just the right time to enable Bristol to take advantage of this global phenomenon.

1. Hadfield and Skimpton, 1979: 240
2. Shannon and Grebenik, 1943: 6
3. Ralph, 1973: 29, Bush, 1976: 115
4. Barry, 2000: 91
5. Buchanan, 2002: 45
6. where the flats at Capricorn Quay now stand
7. now the Arnolfini; Farr, 1977
8. Longmore, 2006: 138
9. Milne, 2006: 259
10. Morgan, 1996: 56-7
11. Minchinton, 1972: 135
12. MacInnes, 1968: 358
13. Nicholls and Taylor, 1882: 309
14. Wells, 1909: 61-2
15. ibid, p 271
16. Neale, 1968: 3
17. Jackson, 1983: 50
18. Longmore, 2006:282
19. Jackson, 1983: 50
20. Jackson 1983: 54-62
21. Bristol was not alone in struggling to generate returns for investors, and even London docks produced disappointing returns, J White, 2007: 183
22. BRO, 08069
23. McGrath, 1975: 159
24. Wells, 1909: 61
25. Bush, 1976: 229
26. Neale, 1968: 5
27. MacInnes, 1968: 361
28. Neale, 1968: 5
29. Bush, 1976: 73
30. *Cosmo's Letters on the Impediments which Obstruct the Trade and Commerce of the City and Port of Bristol*, Bristol Reference Library, BL7E
31. BRO, 08969
32. BRO, M/BCC/DOC/1/14
33. quoted by Wells, 1909, 59
34. ibid: 59-61
35. Bush, 1976: 49
36. ibid, 1976: 166-7
37. Morgan, 1996: 53
38. *Bristol Mercury*, quoted in Nicholls and Taylor, 1882, 312
39. Jarvis 1999: 16-7
40. BRO, PBA/Corp/M/1/2 14 July 1834
41. Wells p65
42. *Municipal Corporations in England and Wales, Appendix to the First Report of the Commissioners, part II*, London: House of Commons, 1835,p 1208-9
43. Common Council Proceedings 1832-1835: 276
44. Proceedings of the Common Council 1832-1835: 308
45. Bush, 1976: 165
46. Wells, 1909: 70
47. ibid, 74
48. ibid, 80
49. Bush, 1976: 167
50. ibid, 170
51. ibid1976: 171, Wells, 1909: 89
52. Jackson, 1983: 125
53. Wells, 1909: 93
54. Neale, 1968: 10
55. Nicholls and Taylor, 1882: 313
56. Neale, 1968: 8
57. Jarvis, 1999: 37

In this chapter we concentrate on the physical performance of the Floating Harbour (as distinct from its economic performance) and the modifications carried out between 1828 and 1834 to make it work better. The grand design conceived by Milton and implemented by Jessop needed only minor structural modification but constant and vigilant management, in particular to deal with the problems posed by deposits of mud. The consultant engineer engaged by the Dock Company to find a solution was Isambard Kingdom Brunel. High profile projects including the Clifton Suspension Bridge, the Great Western Railway and the *Great Britain* (which sits today in the same

dry dock on the Floating Harbour where it was built in the early 1840s) were among Brunel's achievements in Bristol in the 1830s and '40s.[1] It is perhaps less well known that he provided advice to the Dock Company for more than fifteen years, suggesting a number of subtle remedies for problems in the harbour. He also advised on the repair and improvement of one of the entrance locks at Rownham, making it easier for larger ships to enter the harbour.

For half a century after completion of the Floating Harbour there was no development of new quays and no attempt to link the harbour to the railway, which arrived at Temple Meads in 1841. There

The River Frome above the Drawbridge, an open sewer until 1827. (PM slide 5)

Clearing mud from the Harbour, 1828. (T. Rowbotham BMG M2915)

were some new warehouses, such as the Bush Warehouse, built by individual entrepreneurs, but neither the Corporation, which claimed ownership, nor the Society of Merchants, whose lease on the quays continued into the 1840s, made any attempt to improve the facilities of the port. Although we might look back and see the construction of the Floating Harbour as a necessary pre-condition for further development, at the time it appears to have been seen as an end in itself rather than a first step. Instead of pressing ahead to make the most of the investment and to consolidate Bristol's position relative to its competitors, the really striking feature of the history of the next fifty years is how little was done.

The Floating Harbour as a Threat to Public Health

As British cities grew rapidly in the early nineteenth century they all encountered problems of removing human waste and other pollutants. Bristol had disposed of sewage into the tidal river, but of course removing the tide from the harbour just when the population was rising was a recipe for unpleasantness, to say the least. Jessop's optimism about the effectiveness of the bypass sewer included in the works of 1804-9 proved unfounded and the harbour soon became very dirty and smelly. Buchanan[2] pins responsibility for the foul state of the harbour on Jessop's inadequate solution to a foreseeable problem. The Floating Harbour had been the source of complaints for several years before the particularly hot summer of 1825 precipitated action, but not action by the Dock Company, which 'treated appeals for improvement with contemptuous indifference'.[3] It was the Paving Commissioners who took up the matter and in February 1826 the Attorney General obtained an order requiring the Company to make proper provision for removing sewage from the harbour, as was its duty under the Act of 1803. The Company denied liability and it was not until the following year, after further legal action, that the Company agreed to act. Even then the decision was to adopt a solution 'at the least public injury possible and at the most moderate expense'.[4] In view of

The Overfall Dam and the New Cut, 1827. (T. Rowbotham BMG M2931)

the filthy condition of the Floating Harbour it is perhaps surprising that an Act of Parliament in 1822 was required to ban naked bathing between 7am and dusk – a move that was apparently motivated more by concerns about public decency than public health.

Josias Jessop had been retained as consulting engineer to the Dock Company, but he died in 1826 and the directors commissioned William Mylne to devise a suitable plan. In April 1827 he presented a proposal for a culvert from the stone bridge on the Frome (near where an office building called Stonebridge House now stands) running under the harbour at Prince Street Bridge and thence to discharge into the New Cut. The directors accepted the plan and Mylne's Culvert was completed in June 1828, at a cost of £6,276,[5] much to the relief of people living and working adjacent to the Floating Harbour, if not those near the New Cut, which must have been particularly unpleasant at low tide.

The culvert effectively prevented water flowing down the Frome from entering the Floating Harbour, but although it improved the state of the harbour it did not remove the problem of sewage completely for there continued to be complaints. In 1842 one local newspaper referred to the citizens being 'poisoned by the pestilential miasma from [the] stagnant ditch' that was the Floating Harbour.[6]

The Problem of the Mud

Bristol was not unusual in having the problem of mud banks accumulating within the harbour, both clogging the channels and reducing the depth of water at the quays themselves. Large amounts of mud are carried up and down the river Avon, and removing it had always been a problem. Even when the tide regularly washed in and out of the port mud tended to be deposited at points where the current was slack – the slower the movement of the water the smaller the weight of mud that can be held and carried along in suspension. Accumulations of mud were traditionally dealt with by sending in teams of men at low tide to push the mud towards the mainstream so that it would be removed on the next ebb tide. Removing the tidal scouring effect and holding the water at high tide level within the harbour was known to lead to increased silting. It was a problem that had been discussed with William Jessop, who had mentioned dredging as the way to deal with it[7], and as early as September 1809 the Dock Company ordered a steam engine and barge for this purpose.[8] The following May, just a year after the official opening, the Dock Company asked Jessop to propose plans and estimates for scouring the entrances to the harbour where mud accumulated.[9] It seems that although the dredger removed up to 120 tons of mud a day its use was discontinued after only four years, and nothing effective was put in place.[10]

It became established practice to drain the harbour for several days or weeks at a time in order to manually scrape the mud away from the sides. However, by the early 1830s 'large banks or shoals have in the course of several years formed themselves in different parts of the Dock'.[11] And an authoritative report from 1835 made the same point:

> The harbour is now choked with mud. The Act requires 21 feet of water in a sufficient number of berths, but the deepest part now has only 16½, and that only in two berths; it shoals in other parts to 13 and 12. Above the iron swivel-bridge [on the Frome], which may be passed by vessels of 100 tons, are only 10½ in the deepest part, shoaling to eight.[12]

As a result of the accumulations of mud,

> [I]t had been the general practice to lighten all deeply laden vessels in the entrance of the float and notwithstanding this precaution it must be in the recollection of everybody that it was a common sight to see large vessels aground at various shoals in the float and unable without further discharging the cargoes and without great consumption of time, labour and ropes to get up to the Quays.[13]

The Dock Company canvassed ideas for remedies from, among others, John Armstrong, who had worked with Jessop to build the harbour and who was to provide valuable assistance to the man subsequently appointed as consultant engineer to the Company, Isambard Kingdom Brunel. It was in the summer of 1832, when Brunel was just 26 years old, that he was commissioned to report on the state of the harbour. Despite his youthfulness, Brunel already had an established reputation, and the previous year he had won the competition for the proposed Clifton bridge over the Avon Gorge.[14] He was to remain the consultant engineer to both the Dock Company and its successor, the Town Council, until 1849. For reasons unexplained, some accounts of the port of Bristol in the nineteenth century make no reference to Brunel's important work on the problem of the mud in the 1830s.[15] This remedial work was obviously less glamorous than his innovative shipbuilding projects also located in the Floating Harbour, but the long

The drag boat BD6, the second to be built along the lines suggested by Brunel in 1843, still at work in August 1961. (PBAN2731)

term effects were much more enduring and beneficial to the city.

Brunel was a restless innovator, never content to follow conventional solutions if he could come up with something more interesting. His two Bristol ships illustrate the point: having built the world's largest steamship in 1837 he then went on to build a ship, the *Great Britain*, that was twice as big and was criticised by one contemporary as 'a museum of inventions' and 'a congregation of experiments'.[16] In his work on the harbour Brunel was much more cautious and incremental, avoiding grand gestures and expensive untried solutions. He was respectful of Jessop's work and he presented his ideas as modest steps towards realising Jessop's original plan. 'I do not pretend to suggest anything which shall produce any extraordinary effect. The most that I can recommend is to extend and carry more fully into effect the general system upon which the Docks were originally designed'.[17] He also wrote that the shallows and banks were '…not consequences of any fault in the original plans nor of a mere want of scouring power but that partly from a misconception of the intention of Mr Jessop and

partly perhaps from the original designs not having been carried fully into effect by him from motives of economy…'.[18]

What is important about Brunel's analysis and approach is that he did not criticise the basic design of the Floating Harbour. At the macro level Milton's concept and Jessop's realisation of it were confirmed as valid. Brunel was engaged in small-scale adjustments, fine tuning the hydrology so that the harbour would work better. His first report, written within three weeks of being commissioned in August 1832, argued that it was necessary both to remove existing deposits of mud and to adopt measures that would prevent them from re-forming. This required that the harbour should be laid dry to permit manual removal of mud banks, and that then the flow of water through the system should be increased. Simply increasing the current would not wash away existing deposits, but Brunel was confident that the most effective preventive measure required that all the water coming down the Avon should be channelled through the harbour.

The only possible means of preventing deposits is by keeping the whole mass of water in motion…A constant stream though nearly imperceptible in its motion will carry away with it the lighter particles of mud which form the principal part of such deposits. If the whole of the River Avon were at all times running through the float and which I have no doubt Mr Jessop originally intended should be the case such a stream might generally be obtained…[19]

It is unfortunate that such a clear vision was expressed to the directors of the Dock Company in a set of rather ambivalent and even contradictory recommendations. Brunel argued that a culvert through the north pier of Prince Street Bridge was 'indispensable', but that the raising of the height of the Netham Dam was 'of the highest importance though perhaps not altogether indispensable'. This second point is odd, because of the over-riding importance of increasing the flow of water, and the crucial role of Netham Dam in achieving that goal. He

Cumberland Basin entrance locks, from Rownham, between 1865 and 1870, showing Brunel's new lock on the right and Jessop's original north lock on the left. (P 10912)

also proposed a culvert through the Overfall Dam, describing this as 'very desirable [but] by no means absolutely necessary'.

Brunel was not able to inspect the harbour with the water let out until February 1833, but having done so he submitted a second report, with significantly different recommendations. He retained the culvert through Prince Street Bridge, but changed his mind about a similar structure at the Overfall Dam.

For the purposes of drawing off the water at the lower end of the float I do not now think it is necessary to recommend any new culvert through the Overfall Dam but by a very simple arrangement the present culverts may be rendered sufficient…[20]

This very simple arrangement was described by Brunel as a 'trunk' formed by two parallel underwater fences creating between them a ditch through which a fast current of water could be channelled towards the low-level culverts built into the dam by Jessop. It is commonly believed in Bristol that Brunel converted the overfall dam to an underfall by introducing new culverts, but there is no evidence that he did anything more than make greater and more effective use of the structures that were already there.[21] However, by shifting the emphasis from overfall to underfall Brunel made an important contribution to the long-term viability of the harbour, because, as he pointed out, the overfall allowed the cleanest water to escape whereas the underfall sucked out the deepest and therefore muddiest levels of water.

In addition he proposed the acquisition of a 'drag boat'. This was a device for moving banks and shoals by scraping mud into the faster flowing channel so that it would be hydraulically removed from the harbour. These three proposals were costed by Brunel at £2,800, and it is interesting that his suggestions for modifying Netham Dam for a mere £300 were presented as an optional extra. He re-emphasised the importance of increased and constant flow of water into the harbour, but then backed away from insisting on raising the dam:

> *I think that by proper care and management [and] by paying due attention to the draught of the vessels which may at the particular time require to be afloat and to other circumstances the water may almost always be kept much lower than it now is and the inconvenience and expense of any addition to the dam may be obviated. At all events the experiment is worth making as if unsuccessful the expedient of raising the dam may at any time be resorted to.[22]*

This quotation is interesting for two further reasons: first, Brunel displays here his willingness to try something and change it if necessary in the light of experience, and second, lowering the water level within the Floating Harbour was equivalent to raising the dam. Brunel became convinced that the increasing deposits of mud had led harbour managers to raise the water level in order to try to maintain a suitable

The launch of the paddle steamer *Great Western* in 1837, painted in 1919 by Arthur Wilde Parsons. (A. Wilde Parsons BMG K756)

depth, but that this was self defeating. He wanted to lower the bed of the harbour by scouring and then maintain depth by keeping the surface level low enough to sustain a faster current, which would, as he repeatedly argued, prevent silt from being deposited.

The Dock Company adopted Brunel's recommendations for the Prince Street Bridge culvert, the trunk at the Overfall and the drag boat, but they did not raise the Netham Dam nor did they remove the existing mud banks by persistent and effective scouring. In October 1840 a Town Council committee looking at port accommodation noted that '…mud has been allowed to accumulate in the Floating Harbour, particularly above Princes Street Bridge, so as seriously to obstruct the Trade of the Port'.[23] The committee interviewed the Water Bailiff (a council employee responsible for aspects of the harbour upstream from Prince Street Bridge) and was told that the water was only 12 feet deep at the start of his district. He thought that the mud was then 3 feet deeper than it had been 20 years ago, and that there had been no attempt to remove it since he was appointed.[24] Some time later the Dock Company sought another report from Brunel on further measures that might be taken to reduce the amount of mud in the harbour.[25] Brunel treated the directors to a summary of his earlier reports, castigating them for only partially implementing his recommendations. He criticised them for giving in to opposition to scouring from traders who objected to the inconvenience of the harbour being drained. As a result, the structural measures, plus the drag boat, all of which, he now emphasised, were conceived as aids to cleanliness once the mud banks had been removed and the flow of water increased, had come to be relied upon too heavily.[26] He repeated his insistence that ways had to be found to divert the whole of the River Avon into the harbour and that the level of water in the harbour should be kept as low as possible without inconveniencing shipping. He also proposed that to improve the situation in the upper part of the harbour a trunk and culvert should be built at Bathurst Basin, similar to the system at Rownham.

Brunel never criticised the original design of the Floating Harbour. His contribution was confined to minor, and extremely cheap, structural adjustments aimed at improving the flow of water through the harbour, thereby lessening deposits of mud. These were the sorts of fine tuning that were to be expected in a project on this scale, espe-cially bearing in mind the scientific and technological limits within which the construction engineers had been working. Further fine tuning was carried out by the Dock Company's first Superintendent of Works, Joseph Green, who was appointed in 1843 (ie while Brunel was still acting as consultant engineer). In 1846 Green was responsible for restoration work on Brunel's 'trunk', and for covering it in as part of a scheme to reclaim land for workshops, offices and stores.

Brunel's Lock

By comparison with the works carried out by Mylne and Brunel to improve the quality and speed of water flowing through the harbour, the reconstruction and enlargement of the south entrance lock at Cumberland Basin was much more expensive. It was also the first attempt to develop the port infrastructure. For the first few years the Dock Company appears to have spent nothing on repairs, but by the 1830s they were spending at least £1,000 each year on cleaning, and £2-3,000 on repairs. However, in 1839 the cost of repairs jumped to £7,900, and remained above earlier levels thereafter. Between 1846 and 1848 the Company spent a total of £87,000 on repairs, of which £23,800 was due to the work on the south lock.[27]

It was in 1836 that Brunel was asked to report on the repair and possible enlargement of the south entrance lock, the smaller of the two built by Jessop. Some of the masonry was in a very bad state, requiring urgent and complete renewal.[28] There is also a hint in Brunel's report of the impact of technological change, for he referred to 'making such improvements in the entrance generally as the increasing dimensions of vessels, more particularly Steam Boats, and the accommodation of any probable increase of trade may require'.[29] Steam-powered ships had been built in the Floating Harbour since 1822[30] and in 1836 Brunel himself was working on one (the *Great Western*, a paddle steamer launched in 1837 from William Patterson's Wapping yard on the south side of the float). Other ports such as Hull and Liverpool which had locks of comparable size to those in Bristol, were also having to consider the implications of the width of paddle steamers.[31]

The south lock project turned out to be a prolonged and unhappy experience for Brunel, and the last work that he undertook in the Floating Harbour. His report of 1836 outlined four options, the first of which, a simple repair, Brunel regarded as 'almost inadmissable'; the second involved widening the smaller lock to measure 54 feet (but not lengthening it beyond its existing 225 feet[32]), and repairing the north lock; third, widening both locks, taking the smaller one first, and finally he considered widening the lock between the entrance basin and the Floating Harbour itself. In spite of the apparent urgency nothing further was done until Brunel was again called in by the Dock Company in 1843. Only then did the company resolve to go ahead with a rebuilt south lock, 54 feet by 245 feet. Work was put out to tender and contractors began on site in the early part of 1845, but they seem to have been either very inefficient or very thorough, because progress was far too slow for the directors of the Dock Com-

pany, whose relations with Brunel became strained.[33] It was not until 1849 that the rebuilt lock was in working order, which means that this relatively small project had taken four years to complete as compared with five years for the initial construction of the entire Floating Harbour. In these circumstances it was probably a good thing that the Dock Company did not adopt Brunel's more ambitious proposal for rebuilding both locks. This conclusion is reinforced by the operating difficulties associated with Brunel's single leaf caisson gates. By the time the south lock project was complete the Dock Company had been taken over by the Town Council, and further work to improve the locks was not undertaken until the 1870s.

The Shadow of Steam

The Dock Company was under constant financial pressure, and therefore understandably reluctant to go beyond a strict reading of its powers as set out in the Acts of 1803-09. In 1840, for example, the Company wrote to the Town Council's Port Accommodation Committee, 'That it appears to this Board that the Directors have no power whatever to apply any of the Company's Funds towards the providing of additional accommodation for the shipping by extension of the Quay or Wharfs; their duties being confined to the works constructed under the Dock Acts'.[34] The Quay Warden (Mr Claxton, friend of Brunel and also managing director of the Great Western Steamship Company) told the committee that the provision of additional berths for steam ships was absolutely essential, and that it might be possible to create space for two such ships at the Butts (on the Frome). The only other option he could see was to resort to Canon's Marsh although there would be difficulties with access.[35] If there was to be any further development of quay space it would have to come from either the Society of Merchant Venturers under their lease on the existing quays, or private enterprise, but no-one showed any interest. At the time of the construction of the Floating Harbour most of the land adjacent to the impounded area of water remained in private ownership,

The *Great Britain* photographed by W H Fox Talbot in September or October 1844. (D 9069)

and undeveloped. It appears that no-one took any initiative to build new quays for fully fifty years after the opening of the harbour.

However, some important debates took place and decisions were made that had significant long-term implications for the development of Bristol as a port. At the heart of these debates were the emergence of steam ships and the growth of passenger traffic. Early steam-powered vessels tended to be deployed on short routes because their engines were too bulky and inefficient to travel very far without taking on more coal, and it had been argued that it would be impossible to carry enough coal to cross the Atlantic.[36] Brunel's first ship, the *Great Western*, while not the very first steamer to cross the Atlantic was easily the fastest and it pointed to the potential of steam on long-haul routes. However, as Wells has argued, 'We [ie Bristol] lost our supremacy in the Atlantic steamship traffic through mistakes that should have been avoided'.[37] In 1838 the government invited tenders for a contract to carry mail across the Atlantic, and Brunel apparently persuaded the Great Western Steamship Company to bid on the basis of just one ship (the as yet unbuilt *Great Britain*), whereas Samuel Cunard and his backers offered a more regular and reliable service based on a fleet of four paddle steamers.[38] The contract went to Cunard, working out of Liverpool, and the lucrative mail business helped to fuel the growth of that port, much to the chagrin of Bristolians, who continued to blame Brunel for his lack of entrepreneurial skill. Wells, for example, argued that the Great Western Company should have insisted on building three or four more ships like the *Great Western* and that allowing Brunel to go ahead with the *Great Britain* was a fatal error that lost not only the Company but also the port as a whole a lot of money.[39] The *Great Britain* was launched in 1843, but it remained in the Floating Harbour for another eighteen months while fitting out was completed and Brunel negotiated with the Dock Company to enable the great ship to pass through the unreconstructed locks. Once it was completed the vessel lay deep in the water, making it necessary to remove the masonry from the upper part of one side of the lock to allow it to escape, and as is well known it then sailed away, never to

return in its working lifetime. Both the *Great Western* and *Great Britain* sailed out of Liverpool for some years. The irony of all this, of course, is that Brunel and Bristol had given to the world ample evidence that large iron steam ships moved by screw propellers could be made to work successfully over long distances, but Bristol could not take full advantage.

The arrival of transatlantic steam ships in the 1840s coincided with a growth in the numbers of passengers leaving Britain, many of them Irish emigrants, and again Liverpool was well placed to take full advantage. Along with the growth of the size and number of steam ships, mainly carrying passengers, came a debate about where they should be berthed. There were those who argued that large passenger ships did not belong in docks designed for handling cargoes. The *Great Western* was too broad in the beam to enter the Floating Harbour and 'had to lie in Kingroad [outside the mouth of the Avon, in the Bristol Channel] to discharge and load by means of smaller craft'.[40] Nevertheless, the Dock Company insisted on claiming dues as if the ship had entered the harbour, a stance that, not unnaturally, outraged the ship's owners. Plans were discussed for piers at the mouth of the Avon for large passenger ships, but although quite substantial numbers of emigrants were carried from Bristol in the 1840s and '50s the city never established itself as a major passenger port.

Brunel is said to have enthused about carrying the Great Western Railway (GWR) route from London to Bristol onwards to New York by sea, but he was apparently content to have a railway terminus at Temple Meads, some distance from the Floating Harbour, and even further from berths for large passenger ships on the tidal Avon. Although the railway reached Bristol in 1841 it was not extended to the Floating Harbour during Brunel's lifetime. Great visionary engineer that he was, even Brunel did not conceive of the idea of fully integrated transport systems, taking railways to the quaysides to promote the efficient movement of goods. It is arguable that in ports still dominated by sailing ships, which could not be expected to keep to precise timetables, there was no obvious economic advantage in bringing the rails down to the quaysides. Bristol was not alone in the separation of these two key transport networks – both London and Liverpool were also slow to make progress. The people of Bristol were proud of the GWR, which originated with local businessmen perceiving that a rail link to London would be good for trade. However, the GWR acquired, and defended, a monopoly on that route, which was not to the advantage of Bristol traders, and Brunel's idiosyncratic broad gauge system meant that until 1854 goods coming down from the midlands to Bristol for trans-shipment by sea had to be transferred from the standard gauge railway at Gloucester.[41] It is therefore likely that these manufacturers were inclined to send their goods overseas from a northern port.

1. Buchanan, 2002, Kelly and Kelly, 2006
2. Buchanan, 1971: 5
3. Latimer, 1901: 117
4. quoted in Buchanan, 1971: 5
5. BRO, 08969, Dock Company Accounts for 1828
6. quoted in Bush, 1976: 168
7. Hadfield and Skempton, 1979: 231
8. BRO, PBA/Corp/M/1/2
9. ibid
10. *Report of the Commissioners of Municipal Corporations: Bristol, 1835*, p 1207
11. IK Brunel's first report to the Dock Co, August 1832, BRO, PBA/Corp/R/1/1, p1-2
12. *Report of the Commissioners of Municipal Corporations: Bristol, 1835*, p 1207
13. Brunel's report of 1842 BRO, PBA/Corp/R/1/1, p55
14. Buchanan, 2002: 44
15. Reid and Hicks, 1878, Wells, 1909
16. lecture by Mr Scott Russell in 1863, quoted by Nicholls and Taylor, 1882: 312
17. BRO, PBA/Corp/R/1/1, 1832 report, p6
18. ibid, report of February 1833, p19
19. Brunel's first report, p6
20. Brunel's second report, February 1833 p24
21. see for example, Buchanan and Cossons, 1969: 44, Buchanan, 2002: 53, Lord and Southam, 1983: 40, Benbrook, 1989, p20, K White, *A Celebration of the Avon New Cut*, Bristol: Fiducia Press, 2006, p 17
22. ibid, p23
23. BRO, BCC/DOC/3/1, 8 October 1840
24. BRO, BCC/DOC/3/1, Port Accommodation Committee
25. BRO, PBA/Corp/R/1/1, report dated January 1842
26. ibid, p54
27. BRO, 08969, accounts for 1846-48.
28. BRO, PBA/Corp/R/1/1, p40-1
29. ibid, p39
30. Farr, 1977, p37
31. Jackson, 1983: 75
32. Buchanan, 1969, 327
33. Buchanan, 1970, p51
34. BRO, BCC/DOC/3/1, 28 August 1840
35. ibid
36. This claim was made by Dr Dionysius Lardner at a conference in Bristol in 1836, Wells 1909, 69; Burton, 1994, p71
37. Wells, 1909, preface
38. Shipsides and Wall, 1981 p63, Buchanan, 2002, 59
39. Wells, 1909, 76-8, see also MacInnes, 1968: 361
40. Wells, 1909: 69
41. Bird, 1963: 189

St Augustine's Reach below the Drawbridge, about 1890. (PBA N2842)

5 MODERNISING THE PORT

In the second half of the nineteenth century the port of Bristol and the local economy in general prospered, certainly by comparison with the first half.[1] The population of the city and its urban fringe reached 365,000 by 1901[2] and the economy embraced a diverse range of manufacturing industries, employing large numbers of people in tobacco, chocolate, footwear, printing and packaging. One port historian has linked the changing fortunes of the city to the emergence, after 1850, of newly economically powerful families (including the Frys, Wills, Bakers and Robinsons) who made up a new commercial and civic élite, replacing the inbred mercantile community that had held back progress in earlier years.[3] In this context the port was a less significant part of the local economy than it had been a century before. In the hierarchy of British ports Bristol had fallen to 11th place,

Handling a general cargo of boxes, barrels and sacks, Prince's Wharf, August 1948. (PBA 1364)

while its great historical rival, Liverpool, had become second only to London in terms of tonnage.[4] In the period from 1860, while Bristol's passenger numbers declined, Liverpool became the world's leading passenger liner port.[5] However, the diversity of the Bristol economy was to prove an advantage in the longer run, while Liverpool suffered from becoming a more specialised port city.[6]

It is tempting to see the revival of activity in the Floating Harbour as a result of the takeover by the Town Council in 1848, but it is important to remember that there were other factors at work. The achievement of free trade and the repeal of the Navigation Acts in the 1840s gave a great boost to world trade and to the British economy in particular. In the middle of the nineteenth century 40 per cent of the entire world output of traded manufactured goods was produced in Britain, and a quarter of the world's international trade passed through British ports; moreover, by the end of the century Britain had more registered tonnage of ships than the rest of the world put together.[7] In addition to its dominance of international trade the period from 1837 to 1914 was a golden age of British coastal shipping,[8] for which the Floating Harbour was ideally suited.

This context clearly provided enormous scope for Bristol merchants and ship owners to prosper. In 1850 the total tonnage of vessels using the harbour was 643,217, of which 80 per cent was classified as coastal traffic. By 1900 the total had risen to 1,611,730 tons, of which 47 per cent was coastal.[9] So the volume of trade had risen by 150 per cent (albeit that some, no more than 20 per cent, of this increase was accounted for by the new docks at Avonmouth and Portishead, see later), and the pattern had shifted significantly towards foreign imports. It was only from 1893 that foreign tonnage exceeded coastal, and in this respect Bristol was in line with the national trend.[10] Both the volume of traffic and the pattern of movements had implications for the development of the port infrastructure in the form of locks, quays, sheds and railways. From 1859 onwards there was a significant amount of investment in each of these, bringing about a transformation of the Floating Harbour and making it into a modernised port for the industrial era. By 1906, when the goods yard at Canon's Marsh was opened, the modernisation process was effectively complete, a century after the process began. By this date, too, there were nearly 5,000 yards (2.8 miles) of quay and 66,000 square yards of shed space.[11] The working centre of gravity in the Floating Harbour had moved decisively downstream, away from the ancient quays. Indeed, a stretch of the trench originally dug out in the 1240s was covered over and turned into the Tramway Centre (which is why to this day buses still proclaim Centre as their destination).

A complex set of factors (economic growth, local politics, changing cargoes, new technologies) underpinned the development of port facilities in the second half of the nineteenth century. In ports such as Liverpool and London the docks became separated from the city centre partly because of the development of downstream docks but also because of the construction of high walls for improved security against pilfering. 'Liverpool's dock walls were a phenomenon in their own right.'[12] However, the quays on the Floating Harbour mostly remained easily accessible to the public gaze, very much part of the life of the city. Another difference was that in the period 1870 to 1914 Bristol had the highest proportion of shipping entering from abroad but 'clearing coastwise' (going to another UK port).[13] Ships would bring cargoes of timber or wine and then leave empty, en route, perhaps, for south Wales to pick up a load of coal.

Canon's Marsh in 1890, heavily used but not yet developed as quays. (J. Diplock BMG K5538)

...the result was that ships did not remain in Bristol for long or demand extensive facilities for loading cargo....fewer acres of docks could handle more ships because they traded only in one direction.[14]

The Impact of New Technologies

We have seen already how, thanks to Brunel in the 1830s and '40s, Bristol was at the forefront of innovation in ship design, construction and propulsion. However, early steam ships had engines that were low-powered and inefficient, taking up a lot of space onboard and requiring further large amounts of room for fuel. As such they were not suited to the longest sea routes, nor to the carrying of bulk cargoes. Thus sailing ships continued to dominate certain routes, such as those to Australia and the far east. Sail and steam co-existed for several decades – the *Cutty Sark*, for example, was a sailing ship, smaller than the *Great Britain*, but built twenty six years later, in 1869, for bringing tea from China faster than could be achieved by steamer. As the century progressed, however, more iron ships were built, overtaking wooden ones in the late 1860s.[15] Later iron gave way to steel, and steam-engine design advanced, producing much greater efficiency and more power from less bulky engines. It was the perfection of the triple-expansion marine engine after 1880 that really gave a decisive boost to steam-powered shipping,[16] but compared with the rapidity with which the railways spread across the land in the 1830s and '40s it is the slowness of the technological revolution in shipping that is most striking.

Nevertheless, some have argued that the transition to steam was the most significant influence on port business in the period after 1850: 'The associated growth in the size of individual vessels, as also in the quantity of cargoes handled by British ports created a need for additional, more extensive dock, quay and storage accommodation and, in established ports, rendered facilities designed to cater for sailing vessels increasingly outdated and inappropriate'.[17] But what drove technological change? It can be argued that the transition to larger ships, powered by steam, was itself a reflection of deeper social and economic changes. As we have noted, the second half of the nineteenth century saw a large increase in economic activity, driven by free trade and the emergence of an acquisitive and aggressive form of capitalism. Ships earn money only when they are at sea; tied up in port they cost money. It was this that led ship owners to seek to move more goods and people, and to do so faster, working their assets harder. Historically merchants had owned shares in ships, but there was a switch to owning shares in companies that owned ships. This allowed risk to remain spread but concentrated entrepreneurial power in the hands of managers.[18] Examples from Bristol would be the Great Western Steamship Company and the Bristol Steam Navigation Company, both set up in 1836.

The Dockmaster's House, Cumberland Basin, built 1858, demolished for the modern road scheme in the early 1960s. (PBA N2277)

The Drawbridge looking upstream in the 1860s. (P 5155)

We must now say a word about the size of ships, because any general tendency for ships to increase in size represented a grave threat to the viability of the Floating Harbour. There are many references in the literature to the pressure for port modifications due to the increased size of ships. However, there was no sudden and general preference for very large ships. Different markets required different sorts of ships, and it was only in the rapidly expanding business of moving passengers across the oceans that really large ships emerged, and even here Brunel's *Great Eastern*, almost 700 feet in length, and completed in 1858, was exceptional. It was not until the turn of the twentieth century that passenger liners larger than the *Great Eastern* began to slide down the slipways of Belfast and Wallsend. It was not the case that cargo ships followed the same tendency towards gigantism, and ship building survived in Bristol despite the restrictions on the size of vessels that could navigate the river.[19] In Liverpool, which felt the impact of the growth of passenger ships more acutely than anywhere, there was a struggle between passenger-ship owners who wanted expensive investment in long quays with deep water berths, and cargo carriers who believed that the steam ship had already reached an optimum size.[20] It has been claimed that until 1894 the average size of new ships was no more than 1,000 tons,[21] and as late as 1900, 'For every large passenger ship there were perhaps a hundred little tramp steamers bustling around, doing the humdrum work of the world'.[22]

It seems that it was the transition to iron (and later to steel) and steam, rather than increases in size, that had the most impact on the development of the Floating Harbour. By the early 1880s the numbers of steam ships entering the port of Bristol from abroad exceeded those under sail (although in the more significant coastal trade sail still predominated). However, steam ships were, on average, more than twice the tonnage of sailing vessels,[23] so size was not irrelevant. Moreover, 'steamers came and went with such relentless precision that goods could not be brought to or removed from the quays with the necessary speed'.[24] The high cost of constructing steel ships added to the imperative to keep them in port for as little time as possible. Thus

The *Demerara* wrecked in the Avon, 1851. (P 7685)

the emerging dominance of steel and steam had major implications for the development of ports in general, stimulating the provision of both increased storage space at the quayside, and improved means of land transport, principally railways.

'Dockisation' and the Politics of Port Development

Following the takeover by the Town Council in 1848 a majority of the newly constituted Docks Committee had previously served as directors of the Dock Company. From the start the Committee was controlled by people whose business interests lay in the port, including seven merchants and four ship owners.[25] Revenue from the port was below previous years, for three main reasons: cuts in dues in 1848, the adverse impact of the Crimean War and damage to the reputation of Bristol after the newly-launched *Demerara* was wrecked in the Avon in 1851. This ship was as large as the *Great Britain* and the mishap made owners of large ships wary of bringing them up the Avon, and made everyone aware that something should be done to bring the port up to date.[26] During the 1850s there was discussion of a proposed scheme to build a huge new (and ultimately unaffordable) dock at the mouth of the Avon, and then in 1858 the idea of 'dockising' the river by means of a dam at or near its mouth began to be discussed. The docks engineer and supporter of dockisation, Thomas Howard, pointed out to the Docks Committee in 1858 that, 'It is…a striking fact that Bristol, with all her acknowledged advantages, has not one ocean-going steamer trading to foreign ports, while efforts are being made in all parts of the kingdom to meet the increasing requirements of steam navigation…'.[27] Steamers were established on transatlantic routes from the 1840s,[28] and it was the increasing size of passenger liners that contributed to the decline of Bristol as a passenger port in the late 1860s and '70s.[29] In the 1850s and early '60s there had apparently been a flourishing passenger trade taking people

Welsh Back from Bristol Bridge, 1895-1900. (PBA 2304)

from Bristol to Australia, but using sailing ships on such long haul routes on which there were no convenient coaling stations for steamers.[30] It was probably the search for speed and passenger comfort on the transatlantic routes that pushed up the size of liners. But whatever the reason, the rise of huge passenger liners, rather than cargo vessels, reinforced calls for river mouth facilities.

The failure of the Town Council to pursue passenger traffic through investment in docks at the mouth of the Avon eventually prompted two rival private companies to do so. In 1877 Avonmouth dock opened for business, to be followed two years later by Portishead. The two docks were both considerably smaller than the Floating Harbour but they had the advantage of easy access from the sea. Against this had to be weighed the disadvantage of their distance from the city centre, but they had the benefit of being linked by rail to the city and the national network. In this sense they were planned as modern docks, with the transatlantic passenger trade in mind. However, the Town Council competed by cutting the costs of using the Floating Harbour and the two new docks were not commercially successful. The competition for trade and profit was mutually damaging, raising the profile of the port in local politics to a degree that is hard to imagine today.[31] There were many issues that aroused strong opinions, including the burden on ratepayers of subsidies to attract trade up the river, the possibility of the city buying the rival river-mouth docks, the alternative of a non-municipal docks and harbour board to run all three docks (on the model already established for the Mersey), plus of course the ongoing case for dockisation.[32] Eventually the resolution was that the Town Council purchased both Avonmouth and Portishead docks in 1884 for £823,000, which represented a considerable loss for the companies.

From the late 1850s until 1900 developments within the harbour took place in the context of a periodically revived debate between the progressives who favoured dockisation or some other solution at the mouth of the river, and those who remained opposed. This latter group consisted of a loose alliance of people with business interests in

Cumberland Basin, 1929, also showing A and B Bonds, Underfall Yard, the timber yards and Merchants' Dock. (P 9237)

Two divers and other workmen at St Augustine's Reach in the 1890s, probably during the covering of the Frome. (P 9237)

the harbour, who insisted that the City Docks had a future, and those that Neale refers to as the 'fixed property party', a group of councillors with no direct interest in the port and who opposed any investment that would impose an additional burden on the rates.[33] From its inception in 1848 until 1872 the Docks Committee had just two chairmen, Richard Poole King and James Poole, both of whom had their businesses beside the Floating Harbour and were opposed to any river-mouth expansion or development. Subsequently the Committee came to be dominated, from 1875 until 1900, by William Proctor Baker, who was 'the arch-apostle of the City Docks'.[34] He too had substantial business interests beside the water, building on his father's flour milling company in Redcliffe. Baker was responsible for rebuilding one flour mill in 1860, and then adding another next to it in 1862. Twenty years later he built another great mill and granary at Redcliffe, and so he had a lot to defend.

New Quays and Railway Wharves

The first new quay in the Floating Harbour since the eighteenth century was built at Mardyke in 1859 when the Committee seized the opportunity of the widening of Hotwells Road to construct a steamer wharf. Of much greater significance, however, was a proposal for improving the river and harbour put forward in 1864. This was apparently prompted by evidence that a group of private citizens were going ahead with plans to develop a new dock at Avonmouth.[35] An Act of Parliament authorising the plans was obtained in 1865 but it was not until 1873 that the work to improve the locks at Cumberland Basin was finished. A completely new and much enlarged north entrance lock (350 feet by 63 feet) was built to the north west of the old one, which was filled in. The new lock was aligned to make the approach from the river easier, and the new junction lock, of the same size, was also aligned to avoid the sharp turn that ships had previously had to make when entering the float. The southern entrance lock (which had been rebuilt by Brunel) and the old junction lock were not improved

and were subsequently sealed up, but the new locks are still in use today. In addition to the structural improvements to the locks Howard introduced the first hydraulic machinery in the port to open and close the lock gates, which had previously had to be moved manually. This meant that the gates could be opened and closed much more quickly.

Steam cranes at Wapping Railway Wharf, August 1948, loading cargo onto railway trucks. (PBA 1351)

The system was renewed and extended in the 1880s[36] when new workshops and offices for the Harbour Master were created at the Underfall Yard on land reclaimed from the harbour. The hydraulic system is still in use, albeit now powered by electricity rather than steam (and soon to be renewed).

At the same time as the Cumberland Basin works there were plans to extend the railway from the Great Western terminus at Temple Meads to link up with the harbour. As mentioned in chapter 4, Brunel had envisaged a unified rail and sea route from London to New York via Bristol, but the rail terminus at Temple Meads reflected the fact that it was the last available undeveloped site suitable for the purpose, rather than the convenience of its location. The promoters of the GWR

The Gas Ferry in action on an icy Floating Harbour on 20 January 1891, with the Great Western Shipyard in the background.

were Bristol businessmen who were aware of the commercial need to link their city to London and other markets by rail.[37] However, plans to link the railway to the quays were slow to emerge, which was just one of the grievances that Bristol people developed against the company.[38] Others included the lack of a central station and the high cost of sending goods to London: 'In 1862 it was claimed that it was as cheap to send goods to London via Birmingham as to use the GWR route'.[39] By this stage control of the company had shifted to London, and Bristol's interests could not always be defended (to make matters worse from the Bristol point of view, there was a significant group of shareholders from Liverpool, perhaps reflecting the tendency for compensation paid to slave owners after abolition in 1834 to be invested in railways). For whatever reason, the GWR showed no great enthusiasm for or sense of urgency about developing a good harbour railway. In fairness to the GWR, Bristol was not unusual in the slow emergence of good port-rail links.[40]

This continued to be the company's stance through to the end of the century as the GWR seemed to be more concerned to protect its virtual monopoly position.[41] In 1883, for example, the company strenuously opposed a radical scheme to both bring railways to the harbour and establish a second route to London. This would have involved constructing a central station by covering the Frome between the Drawbridge and the Stone Bridge. Despite popular support within the city this scheme was defeated.[42] It also seems reasonable to conclude that the GWR agreed to co-operate on plans to extend the railway round to Canon's Marsh in the 1890s only once it became clear that the Midland Railway were not going to be involved.

The first attempt to link the harbour to the main railway line was in 1861, and would have involved a station at Queen Square and a terminus at Brandon Hill, implying two crossings of the water.[43] Opposition defeated both this plan and the proposals in the Bristol Port Extension Railway Act, 1864, which included a route along the right bank of the float, along the Back, turning right along the Grove to a terminus at Prince Street.[44] In 1866 the Bristol Harbour Railway

The Albion Dockyard and timber yards at Baltic Wharf, early 1900s. (P 4367)

Act (promoted by the GWR and Bristol and Exeter Railway) did lead to a major development on the water side at Wapping. The area to the west of Bathurst Basin was then occupied by a complex and shifting set of ship yards and dry docks, in multiple private ownership. So complex was the ownership of the land, and so heavily worked was the assembled site that straightening the edge for the new wall and levelling the surface for railway tracks must have been a major undertaking.

Under the 1866 Act the Council acquired land and built just over 300 yards of wharf either side of Wapping Road in about 1868 (now known as Wapping and Prince's Wharfs).[45] The railway companies then built a railway from Temple Meads, involving a bridge over the road to the west of the station, a 282-yard tunnel, passing under a corner of St Mary Redcliffe churchyard, and a bridge across the entrance to Bathurst Basin – which indicates the difficulty of extending the railway to the harbour.

The first railway wharf was not particularly convenient and in 1873 a second Act enabled the Council and the railway companies to bring the rails closer to the water by constructing another, the Wapping Railway Wharf, from the 35-ton steam crane (1875) along to Wapping Dry Dock (where the *Great Britain* sits). There were 11 railway sidings on the extended railway wharf. The land between

Canon's Marsh seen from the roof of the Corporation Granary about 1900, showing timber yards and marble works. (D 375)

Wapping Road and the crane was owned by the Council and here it later built the huge Corporation Granary in 1888. This building, which dominated the view down St Augustine's reach, reflected the growth of grain imports (1887-1895 imports of grain into the City Docks rose from 200,000 to 570,000 tons).[46] Bulk cargoes on this scale demanded mechanised means of unloading, and the granary was connected to the port's hydraulic system.

The Bathurst and Prince's railway wharves added nearly 1,000 yards of stone-walled quayside. But this was only the start of a phase of active debate about ways of developing yet more space in the 1880s and '90s. There were two large and promising sites, Canon's Marsh and the area now referred to as Baltic Wharf but then known by six distinct names.[47] The problem was that neither was close enough to the railway. Objecting to Canon's Marsh in 1885 Alderman Proctor Baker cited both the extra haulage costs due to the lack of rail connection, and the decline in trade over the period since 1877.[48] The reply he received is revealing: 'The General Manager pointed out that the trade practically was now all done by steamers instead of sailing craft. The former required to discharge goods with great speed and therefore required much more quay space than 8 years ago when sailing craft stayed at general berths often two off [ie double parked, waiting for a place at the quayside] for days or weeks together. The trade demanded better accommodation than then.'[49]

There were already plans to extend the rails still further so as to serve the timber yards beyond the Albion Dockyard. This area had been used mainly as pasture but since the mid-1850s it had been taken over for ship building and timber stacking.[50] There were plans to provide 500 yards of stone quays fronting the 20-acre site. It was also proposed to replace the timber yards with coal tips as a strategy for developing a coal exporting trade. But the railways never arrived and the timber yards remained in place. Again, difficulties in reaching agreement with the GWR seem to have been the stumbling block. An experimental coal tip at Cabbage Gardens (at Cumberland Basin)[51] featured in another proposal, in 1889, when the Council approved

plans to extend the railway to Cumberland Basin, with sidings for the timber wharfs and the Irish cattle trade. But the Bill was withdrawn because of failure to reach agreement with GWR.

In 1892 the Docks Committee revived the plan and included a swing bridge across the New Cut downstream from the Underfall, subject to agreement with GWR. The new bridge would link the harbour railway to the main line and Portishead Dock. The plan failed again but was revived in an expanded form in 1895, including a scheme to build 500 yards of timber wharf from Hill's yard to Cumberland Basin. This was apparently urgently needed in order to relieve pressure on quays elsewhere in the harbour, but the scheme was not completed as planned, despite the council spending £70,000 buying 12 acres of land west of the Albion Dockyard in 1900.[52] The proposed rail link could not be agreed, and the GWR went ahead with a different option, running a track along the side of the New Cut to sidings at Cumberland Basin.

In relation to Canon's Marsh, it was resolved in May 1885 that it was essential that extended quay, rail and storage provision should be made available on this large and undeveloped site.[53] Discussions were opened with the railway companies. At the same time it was recognised that it would be expedient to purchase the whole of the frontage from St Augustine's round to the Gas Works. Work was underway in 1892 at the Butts and Dean's Marsh to improve access and provide both quays and sheds.[54] The work to develop the quay and sheds on the right bank of the Frome was not straightforward, for it involved filling in an existing dry dock and removing the remains of bodies buried in the churchyard of St Augustine-the-Less (all trace of this church has now disappeared). The Docks Committee tried repeatedly but unsuccessfully to persuade the Midland Railway to develop a goods yard at Canon's Marsh, and in the process a number of possible routes in were explored to avoid crossing the harbour. The pursuit of the Midland Railway was doubtless motivated by a desire to stiffen competition with the GWR. Equally, the GWR's apparent reluctance to develop the port through improved rail links has been attributed

A post-1945 view of Ashton Swing Bridge over the New Cut, with the railway carried below the road. (P 12709)

means of a line extending from the newly constructed Ashton Swing Bridge, swinging to the right and then left to cross the Cumberland Basin junction locks. It then went up the western side of Merchants' Dock, which was partially filled in to accommodate the need to make a sharp right turn so as to run along the side of the harbour at Mardyke, then behind the gas works and into Canon's Marsh. It must have been a slow journey for trains once they left the main line. By the time the scheme was complete in 1906 the railway fanned out across Canon's Marsh and linked up with the transit sheds on the waterside. It was a fine facility, but as Neale observes, 'the whole scheme, dock sheds at Canon's Marsh included, could well have come at least ten years earlier'.[57]

Creating the 'Centre'

In 1887 debate began about replacing the existing drawbridge across the Frome opposite the end of Baldwin Street. The drawbridge was only 20 years old but the increase in road traffic was such that there was a demand for a fixed bridge. The fact that this was successful is also a sign of how the centre of gravity in the harbour had shifted downstream, away from the ancient quays. The upstream arm of the harbour had long been associated with, and really only accessible by, small flat-bottomed boats called Severn trows, but the economic power now lay with the owners of larger steam vessels and with shore-based vehicles. A fixed bridge would be part of an important cross-city route, making it much easier to get from Clifton to Temple Meads, and it was an obvious development to the route that had already been improved by straightening Baldwin Street. The new fixed bridge was completed in 1893, and the river upstream to the Stone Bridge was then culverted. The reclaimed land was initially used for a temporary exhibition hall, and then much of it was laid out as gardens. It was here, too, that the Bristol Tramway Company established the Tramway Centre at the hub of its network when electric trams were introduced in 1895.

to its determination to keep the Midland Railway from close contact with the docks.[55] Eventually, when it became clear that the Midland could not be persuaded it was resolved that every effort should be made to win over the GWR. Finally, in 1896 a Bill was successfully promoted and, 'Seeing that at last Bristol was in earnest, the Great Western Railway Company decided to make a large railway depot at Canon's Marsh'.[56] The GWR would now control railway access to virtually the whole of the Floating Harbour, while the Midland had only limited and poor-quality access via its goods yard at Cuckold's Pill, upstream from Bristol Bridge and therefore accessible only by barges.

The attraction of Canon's Marsh as a goods yard was that it was a large area of flat ground abutting the water on two sides, but the problem was getting the railway lines in there. This was achieved by

1893 filling-in of the Frome to create the Centre, with St Mary-on-the-Quay to the right. (D 9534)

From Floating Harbour to City Docks

The opening of the Canon's Marsh goods yard in 1906, almost exactly 100 years after the construction of the Floating Harbour, and half way through our story, is a good point at which to take stock. Much had changed since the night that the labourers' feast in the field at Wapping ended in a memorable brawl. A triumph in engineering terms though the Floating Harbour was, it nevertheless seemed as if the financial burden might actually kill off the port. It was in effect rescued from failure by the enormous growth of the British economy as a whole, only then to be threatened by technological change. Despite the criticism heaped on the Dock Company the port was still viable when it was taken over by the Town Council. This seems to have been a crucial development, because it was only then that investment in developing the physical infrastructure began to pick up. The City Docks of 1906 represented a transformation achieved in less than half a century: new entrance locks, much extended quays, extensive amounts of shed space for storing goods and railways for moving them on quickly. The authorities now owned a lot more of the land around the water, but there remained some private wharves and yards as well as the general public quays. One recent development was that some shipping lines were demanding their own dedicated berths and sheds on parts of the public quays.

The river route up to Bristol had been improved and within the harbour there were also new and reconstructed bridges. The Docks in 1906 had completed a transition to the industrial era. There was little space left for development – the quayside at Baltic Wharf was never built up to the height that was normal elsewhere, and deep-water berths were never established, nor did it get its rail link. But the rest of the available space was taken up. The sacrificing of the top section of the Frome arm of the harbour was not a great loss by that stage, because during the nineteenth century there was a gradual but significant downstream movement of port activity within the docks. After 500 years the ancient quays had lost much of their former im-

portance. In particular the downstream tendency had transformed the Wapping side of the float; here and elsewhere within the harbour shipyards were lost to wharf building. Although ship building continued well into the new century there were fewer sites available.

A major contrast between the Dock Company and the Town Council was the proactive role played by the Council and its Docks Committee, not just in terms of the development of the infrastructure but also in the promotion of new business by means of targeted investment. In the past the authorities had simply provided facilities for ships to tie up, and had charged their owners for the privilege of moving cargo through the port. But in the second half of the nineteenth century the Committee actively pursued ways of expanding the trade of the port by investing in specific ventures, such as the Corporation Granary and the idea of an experimental coal tip at Cumberland Basin as a way of promoting exports from the local coalfields. Perhaps the most significant example was the decision in 1902 to build two huge

Mardyke ferry, February 1961, with HMS *Flying Fox* in the background. (PBA N2527)

bonded warehouses at Cabbage Gardens for tobacco imports. The newly formed Imperial Tobacco had indicated a decision to import raw materials direct to Bristol but it was not legally allowed to build its own bonded warehouses, so the Council built them, facilitating the long-term growth of an important business in the city. The tobacco bonds were just the most visible evidence of the Docks Committee's pursuit of new business; for example in 1906 the port's general manager, Mr Francis Girdlestone, spent several weeks in Canada and the United States promoting the attractions of Bristol.[58]

Finally, we have referred to the struggle between those who favoured the development of river-mouth docks or dockisation and defenders of the Floating Harbour. There is a global tendency for docks to move away from crowded ancient ports and down towards the sea and deep water, but the story of the Floating Harbour suggests that those who championed the development of the city centre site were not wrong to do so. At the start of the twentieth century the City Docks were still doing more business than Portishead and Avonmouth put together, and the years 1911-1914 were the busiest ever.

1. Ollerenshaw and Wardley 1996
2. Shannon and Grebenik
3. Neale, 1968: 30
4. Jackson, G, 1988: 246-9
5. Milne, 2006: 260
6. ibid: 264
7. Mathias, 1983: 229 and 286
8. Bagwell and Armstrong, 1988: 171
9. BRO, M/BCC/DOC/1/14 Bristol Docks Statement of Accounts for the year to 30 April 1915
10. Bagwell and Armstrong, 1988: 173
11. Port of Bristol Official Handbook, 1906, p11. Liverpool then had 36 miles of quays – BRO, M/BCC/DOC/1/10, Bristol Docks Committee, Reports of Officers etc, 1914, vol. 1
12. Milne, 2006: 269
13. Jackson, 1983: 125
14. ibid: 125-6
15. Burton, 1994; 97
16. ibid, p103
17. Palmer, in Daunton, 2000: 142
18. Murphy, 1973: 540; Jackson, 1988: 255-6
19. Farr, 1977
20. Hyde, 1971: 115
21. Murphy, 1973: 539
22. Burton, 1994: 164
23. Large, 1984: xxiv, table X
24. Jackson, 1988: 224
25. Neale, 1968: 9
26. Wells, 1909: 106
27. quoted by Wells, 1909: 136
28. Harley, 1971, 222
29. MacInnes, 1968, 427
30. ibid, p422-3
31. The same point has been made about Liverpool in the nineteenth century, Milne, 2006: 281
32. Wells, 1909, chapter 10, Neale, 1968
33. Neale, 1968: 10-11
34. Neale, 1968: 16
35. Wells, 1909: 158
36. Buchanan, 1971: 16
37. Channon, 1985: 2
38. Gibson, 2002: 10
39. ibid, p10
40. Jackson, 1988: 224-5
41. Neale, 1970: 59
42. Wells, 1909: 372
43. Wells, 1909: 365, Vincent, 1979: 9
44. BRO, Dock Plans, roll 10, 07783(12)9
45. BRO, BCC/D/PBA/Corp/E/3/179a
46. Neale, 1968: 17
47. Maps from the 1880s identify, from west to east, Baltic, Onega, Cumberland, Canada, Gefle (a corruption of Gavle, a port in Sweden) and Chatham
48. BRO, PBA/Corp/M/3/2
49. ibid, 13 March
50. Lord and Southam, 1983: 87
51. Wells, 1909: 273
52. Neale, 1970: 58
53. BRO, PBA/Corp/M/3/2, 5 May
54. BRO, PBA/Corp/M/3/9, 4 January
55. Neale, 1970: 59
56. Wells, 1909: 302
57. Neale, 1970: 94
58. Wells, 1909: 409

6 THE FLOATING HARBOUR IN WAR AND PEACE

The story of the Floating Harbour in the nineteenth century shows how the huge cost of construction imposed a financial burden on the port that was justified and made bearable only by wider economic growth later in the century. The Floating Harbour was a local project validated by national and global trends. In the twentieth century it was the other way round. No matter what the local decision-makers did global trends eventually killed off the Floating Harbour as a commercially viable port. Whereas in the later nineteenth century, trade passing through the Floating Harbour justified continued investment, in the twentieth century it was necessary to adapt to a significantly more difficult environment. Bristol was not alone in having to come to terms with inexorable change, and a leading port historian has depicted the period 1919-1980 as one of 'stagnation and decay' for British ports in general.[1]

Of course as the Floating Harbour reached its centenary in 1909 all this lay in the future, and although Britain's share of world shipping was already falling, there was no real sign of the threats that lay ahead. In fact the years immediately before the First World War were the best ever for the Floating Harbour, which still conducted more business than both Avonmouth and Portishead put together. One measure of activity is that in 1913 6,600 vessels entered the Floating Harbour.[2] The City Docks remained at the heart of the Port of Bristol, and as such it was a complex and integral part of urban Bristol and its local economy. The Floating Harbour was still central to the way Bristolians thought of their city. At one level it consisted of a set of waterways, locks, quaysides, sheds, warehouses, roads and railways – a busy and constantly changing scene familiar and visible to all. One eyewitness account of the harbour before 1914 talks of the boats and ships graduated in size along the quays below Bristol Bridge, with the smaller ones furthest upstream. These were coasters, both sail and steam, from South Wales and other Bristol Channel ports. Then

Loading coke at the Gas Works jetty, June 1952, with the Great Western Dry Dock in the background. (PBA 1838)

came larger vessels, from Liverpool, Glasgow and the east coast ports. 'Along the Grove inset with old square bays, the larger coastal liners from London, Liverpool and Manchester mostly lay. The ships along the length of the Narrow and Broad Quays were a less settled lot, foreign-going ships, coasters, barges, though at the City end the Bristol Steam Navigation Company plied their Cork, Waterford and other Irish trade.'[3] The account goes on to mention cattle being driven from these Irish ships onto the quayside 'within a bellow of…the branch offices of leading insurance companies'.

The Port was also a set of individuals, companies and other organisations all co-operating or competing with each other. The Council owned the docks but it did not own all the wharves and quays, nor all the land around the water; there were still substantial lengths of waterfront in private ownership, notably the western stretch of Canon's Marsh and the Redcliffe side of the Avon below Bristol Bridge. Most of the economic activity that took place was carried out by private firms: ship owners, shipping agents, stevedoring companies, importers and exporters, ship builders and repairers, ships' chandlers and shore-based transport companies. Large numbers of jobs and a substantial proportion of the local and regional economy depended on the docks, still dominated by the City Docks, and it was the role of the Docks Committee to support private enterprise. This meant making sure that ships could come and go as the tides permitted and market forces demanded, loading and unloading as efficiently as possible, and that goods could be stored before being moved from the quaysides. None of the major UK ports was run for profit: their authorities saw their role as to enable others to make profits. Bristol differed only in that it was run by the Town Council whereas London, Liverpool and a majority of others were managed by non-profit making trusts made up of representatives of the various interests involved in the port. However, some important ports, including Hull and Southampton, and some of Bristol's direct competitors, such as Newport and Fishguard, were controlled by railway companies,[4] a fact which gave rise to a good deal of resentment at the Port of Bristol.

Taking delivery of Italian potatoes at A Shed, May 1955. (PBA N296)

The Docks Committee and the managers they employed to run the port were never in complete control. Although they could drum up trade to some extent and they could attract vessels by developing new and better facilities, the authorities in Bristol and other ports were always in the position of responding to changes rather than driving them. Shippers could shift their business to rival ports, or at least threaten to do so. New kinds of ships, especially larger ships, carrying different cargoes and requiring different handling methods posed difficult challenges.

The Dockers Find a Voice

A hundred years ago when Charles Wells wrote his *Short History of the Port of Bristol* (which actually ran to more than 400 pages) he gave considerable attention to the leading decision makers and power brokers in the city, the members of the Dock Company and subsequently the councillors on the Docks Committee, plus the

Preparing to unload Russian timber at Baltic Wharf, October 1938. Failure to raise the quay wall meant that ships had to stand off, creating extra work and hazard for dockers. (PBA 833)

engineers who had built and modified the Floating Harbour. But he made virtually no reference to the people who spent their working lives in the docks, heaving cargoes on and off ships or driving laden carts and trains. Dock work involved hard manual labour but it was poorly paid and insecure. The main qualification for the work was physical strength and stamina. Historically dock work had been subject to marked seasonal variations, reflecting harvest times and sea conditions (for example, timber imports into Bristol generally arrived between April and November). The twin factors of low skill requirements and insecurity of employment meant that it was difficult to organise the men into trade unions (which flourished among craft-based industrial manufacturing workers).

However, in 1889 an epoch-making five-week strike by London dockers provided the impetus for a sustainable dockers' union. The Dock, Wharf, Riverside and General Workers' Union was set up by a Bristolian, Ben Tillett, but ironically in Bristol, although there was a brief dock strike in the wake of the London dispute, the workers apparently continued at first to let the Gasworkers' Union represent their interests.[5] Membership fell after 1892[6] but Tillett was a persuasive orator and in due course Bristol and the other ports on the Bristol Channel became the stronghold of his union.[7] One of the recruits to the union was the young Ernest Bevin, who, in 1910, was working as a mineral water delivery driver for a firm in St Paul's.[8] This was a period of renewed industrial conflict and trade union growth as workers sought to benefit from economic recovery after high unemployment in 1908 and 1909. Bevin formed a carters' branch of the Dockers' Union. He went on to become a full-time employee of the Union in 1911 and a key player in negotiations between the Bristol docks' employers and workers until after the First World War. A decade later Bevin played an important part in the creation of the Transport and General Workers' Union, of which he was the first general secretary representing 300,000 workers (he was later Minster of Labour in Churchill's war cabinet and then Foreign Secretary in the 1945 Labour government).

Bevin was just one of 2,000 new members signed up by the Dockers' Union in 1910 in a period of growing tension between employers and workers that saw numerous disputes and strikes over the next three years. The national membership of the Union rose by 250% between 1910 and 1914, and although there are no reliable local figures the evidence of rising income suggests that growth was in line with the national trend.[9] One distinguishing feature of the Bristol membership, however, was that carters, other road transport workers and general labourers were signed up in greater numbers than elsewhere,[10] giving their negotiators a stronger hand.

One of their issues was the decasualisation of dock labour. The dockers were employed only as and when there was work for them to do, and of course sometimes there was nothing while at other times there was a glut. Casual work was associated with a demeaning

Inside A Bond, 1920, weighing and sampling imported tobacco. (PBA 208)

The diminutive river tug *Volunteer* tows the Baltic steamer *Star* outbound through Cumberland Basin about 1937. (POS 62)

daily scrummage as dockers competed to catch the eye of employers willing to hire them. In the City Docks it was quite usual for workers to be hired at the ship's side or transit shed.[11] The first steps towards decasualisation were taken in Liverpool in 1912, when a registration scheme was introduced. A partial decasualisation scheme for Bristol followed in 1919, when Bevin and the port's general manager, Dennis Ross-Johnson, devised a registration scheme for Bristol dockers, giving some 3,600 registered dockers the guarantee of more regular work by the exclusion of non-registered men. It has been claimed that thanks to Bevin and the strength of the Union locally the Bristol scheme offered more favourable conditions than similar ones elsewhere.[12] However, registration was only the first step: 'the next problem, no less important, [was] to distribute the volume of registered labour in accordance with the constantly changing demand for it'.[13] Decasualisation meant regular work for a smaller number of dockers. It has to be admitted that not all dock workers yearned for the end of casual employment,

for it had certain advantages, particularly the freedom not to work a full week every week, and the registration scheme did imply that the men would accept a greater degree of flexibility in the activities they undertook. In the event decasualisation was very slow to be achieved, and the regular competition for work carried on until the last days of commercial activity in the City Docks in the 1960s.

The fact that dockers were casual workers meant that it is difficult to know how many there were altogether, but one estimate is that in 1914 there were 2,850 in the Port of Bristol as a whole.[14] Most were what might be called 'regular casuals', those who saw dock work as their main or only source of income, but there were irregular casuals who would turn up when there was plenty of dock work and/or not much available elsewhere. Some figures from 1933 show just how variable could be the demand for labour: the maximum number of casual workers employed on any one day in that year was 2,911, while the minimum was just 400.[15] 'There can be no doubt but that there were hard times in the homes of most of the regular casuals when trade at the docks was slack…'.[16] Such workers were earning no more than £100 per year in 1914 (equivalent to about £8,500 today), and we know that Bevin was paid much the same, £2 per week, when he became a union organiser in 1911.[17] However, for a docker to reach £100 per year he would have needed to work a full week every week, which most did not or could not achieve. One estimate is that before 1914 casual dockers worked on average two and a half or three days a week.[18]

The simple term 'docker' conceals the complexity of the occupational structure of the docks. The Port of Bristol employed only about 600 permanent staff, plus a number of casual dockers working at the Corporation Granary, but in general the loading and unloading of ships was carried out by private firms of stevedores by arrangement with the owners or agents of vessels using the port.[19] Paul Elkin has argued that 'the distinction between 'dockers' and 'stevedores' is an important one. Although working practices could vary greatly between different parts of the country, dockers were traditionally employed in

Bristol as elsewhere on an entirely casual basis only when there were vessels to be unloaded or loaded. Paid by the day by a port's managing authority, dockers provided the basic manpower still essential for most cargo handling…Stevedores, on the other hand, although performing much the same heavy lifting and man-handling of cargoes as dockers, were employed usually on a weekly basis by private companies which operated under licence in the port to provide ship owners and agents with a more skilled manual workforce specifically responsible for the actual loading and distribution of cargo within the holds of a ship and sometimes within warehouses or transit sheds when more careful handling of a load was required than the average docker might be expected to give.'[20]

It is reasonable to assume that men who were regarded as reliable and steady workers would be in a good position to secure regular casual work and, to some extent, to be able to specialise in particular types of cargo. Some cargoes, such as bulk grains, required dockers to work in small teams, some shovelling while others bagged and carried the sacks out of the hold to be weighed. Some dockers sought to define themselves as, for example, deal-runners (unloading timber) or coal-trimmers, while others had to settle for general labourer. Different roles and different cargoes attracted different rates of pay, creating complex administrative problems.

One of the consequences of the war was a high level of inflation, which doubled the price of goods between 1914 and 1918. By 1919 the nominal value of dock workers' pay had risen from 7d per hour in 1914 to 1s-9d.[21] In 1916 it was agreed between the principal employers and the representatives of the workers that employers would hire only members of the Union, and in return the Union undertook to urge its members to work full time.[22] There was, however, a significant fall in output per man, which has been estimated to be 20-30 per cent between 1914 and 1919.[23] Part of the explanation may be that the younger, fitter and most productive dockers were the ones most likely to have gone off to the war.

There were numerous small and mostly brief stoppages of work as dockers and their employers disputed terms and conditions, but the power of the Union was most dramatically displayed in the General Strike of May 1926. When the coal miners struck over attempts to cut their pay and increase working hours the TUC called out workers in other key sectors of the economy, including railways and docks. Bristol dockers not only supported the strike but stayed out for more than a week beyond the official return to work.[24] However, the docks were not at a complete standstill for some movement of cargoes was organised by the employers mobilising volunteer labour. Thereafter, in Bristol and the rest of the country, the power of the unions was much reduced and the number of days lost to industrial disputes fell steeply.

Two outbound steamers entering Cumberland Basin watched by a barge crew in 1937. (POS 229)

The Changing Governance of the Docks

The emerging power of the dockers' union was just one indication of how the governance of the port was changing. Another key indicator was the declining numbers of Docks Committee members with direct business interests in or around the Floating Harbour. After the influence wielded in the 1890s by Alderman Proctor Baker this must have been very noticeable at the time. In the early 1880s two thirds of the Committee had their principal business interests in trade or industry directly related to the port,[25] but four decades later out of the twenty six individuals who at various times constituted the Docks Committee in the inter-war period just three, Frederick C Burgess, Mark Whitwill and Charles Hartly Hodder, had a direct commercial interest in the port and only two could be said to have any related interest.[26]

Part of the explanation might be that this was a reflection of a more general trend as local business leaders began to drop out of local politics. A more specific factor might be the decision in 1911 to cut the numbers of Docks Committee members from 20 to 11. Nevertheless there were some important strands of continuity on the Committee, with Alderman Twiggs occupying the chair from 1908 to 1924, having served from 1890 (with a four-year break, 1896-1900), and Alderman Sir William Howell Davies who served from 1887 to 1931. They were not the only long-serving members, but more eye-catching perhaps is the appearance of representatives of the working class (though not necessarily dock workers themselves) in the form of Labour councillors who began to be admitted to the Committee in 1913. The first was Walter Ayles who served on the Committee until 1922 (he went on to become MP for Bristol North). The Labour Party gradually increased its strength on the Council and the Docks Committee to the point when, in 1937, Alderman A Burgess became the first Labour chairman of the Committee.[27]

The elected members of the council who constituted the Committee naturally depended on their salaried staff to advise them and to carry out their policies. An important change occurred in 1911

Tug towing two paper pulp-laden barges down St Augustine's Reach, August 1948. (PBA 1345)

when Francis Girdlestone retired as general secretary and manager after 36 years' service. He was replaced by Dennis Ross-Johnson, who remained in post for 20 years, during which time he introduced a series of important innovations and improvements in the management and operation of the port.

It has been claimed by Kieran Kelly that between the two world wars the Docks Committee operated largely independently of the Council, and that its strategy was commercial in approach.[28] These two features are, of course, not unrelated. The Docks Committee was running what was in effect a major business, responsible for millions of pounds worth of investment and thousands of jobs in the local economy. As a municipal trading service it was quite different from, for example, education or refuse collection, which were free services

Launch of the *Boston City* from Albion Dockyard, 1917. (D9271)

Manhandling general cargo at T shed, September 1946. (PBA 1031)

Barrels of Portuguese wine and Spanish sherry in U shed, 1961. (PBA N2832)

the docks were on a generally downwards trajectory, falling from £129,500 in 1913 to £25,000 by 1939.[32] It should be remembered here that the Council was still benefiting from the collection of City Dues (until 1932), which to some extent offset expenditure on the docks. One of the reasons for rates contribution was the heavy obligations placed on Bristol to provide for debt redemption through a 'sinking fund'; as a municipal undertaking the rules governing sinking fund payments were said to be significantly more onerous than those on other ports. This was something that was frequently cited as an example of the unfairness of the terms on which Bristol was competing with other ports.[33] Another was the allegation that Bristol was at a disadvantage compared with railway-owned ports. It was argued that railway companies offered cut-price rates for goods moved through their ports, making their profits on the movement of goods by rail to and from those ports.[34] Bristol claimed to have lost significant amounts of live cattle trade with Ireland as a result of competition of this sort from the railway-owned port of Fishguard.

Patterns of Trade

Bristol had always been a general cargo port, as distinct from specialist coal ports such as Newport and Cardiff. It was also unlike these ports in that its business was dominated by imports. The types of cargo coming into Bristol changed over time, although grain, timber, sugar and tobacco remained important. The outbreak of war in August 1914 marked a turning point for the Floating Harbour, which had enjoyed a run of several years when the volume of cargo had exceeded two million tons.[35] It turned out that the year to April 1914 was the best ever in terms of the tonnage of goods through the Floating Harbour. During the war years the weight of goods traded through the City Docks fell by nearly two thirds, partly because of the diversion of men and ships to the war effort and partly because of the effective blockade of British ports by enemy submarines.

Although there was a post-war recovery in trade through the City

paid for entirely out of rates income. However, Kelly argues that there was a distinct 'transition from an ethos of local service to a more commercial orientation'[29] which was used as a way of maintaining independence from the council. One symbolic indicator of this independence was the decision, in 1925, to adopt the title 'Port of Bristol Authority'.[30] This decision, which was made without reference to the council, suggests an independent entity, separate from the council, and may have been adopted to mimic the Port of London Authority, which had been set up in 1909.

According to Kelly, an important aspect of the increasing commercial orientation of the Docks Committee was the priority attached to reducing the subsidy from the ratepayers. He argues that 'By the inter-war years…the Port of Bristol was run in a manner that put the interests of the dock enterprise before any local sectional interest…the business interests of the Port were allowed to override what might have been seen as the economic interests of local firms and local labour'.[31] It is certainly true that rates contributions towards

Docks it never managed to approach the volumes achieved in 1911-1914. Before the war bulk grain imports were the main cargo entering Bristol, a third of which, approaching 300,000 tons, came into the Floating Harbour (as a result of Alderman Proctor Baker's efforts in the 1890s), but by 1918 less than 12,000 tons found their way up the Avon. Although the figures rose in later years the balance had shifted irrevocably to Avonmouth, and by 1932 Spiller's (which had merged with Baker's) were seeking to move their milling business out of Redcliffe and into Avonmouth.[36] Other staple imports such as timber, tobacco and sugar also suffered steep falls during the war, only to partially recover later.

The two decades between the wars are often thought of as times of great economic hardship and high unemployment. While it is true that there were periods of economic difficulty, and certain industries, notably mining, ship building and heavy engineering, suffered acutely, it is a mistake to think that all regions and all parts of the economy were in trouble all the time. Immediately after the Armistice of November 1918 there was a brief economic boom, which turned into a recession in 1922, and thereafter unemployment remained relatively high throughout the period up to 1939, with a severe peak in 1932. Economic recovery boosted trade until 1929 and the onset of the Great Depression sparked by the Wall Street Crash. By the mid-1930s the economy was recovering, and for those who were in employment living standards were rising. New industries, such as vehicle and aircraft manufacturing, were prospering, and Bristol was much less badly affected than some of the northern cities with which its critics had drawn negative comparisons a century earlier.

After the war Britain's export markets were much reduced and coastal trade, which was so important for Bristol's Floating Harbour, fell by 30 per cent.[37] The inter-war period saw the beginning of the long decline for coastal shipping as shore-based transport systems, both road and rail, competed more effectively. In the case of the Floating Harbour, there are two general points to be made. First, it never recovered its share of pre-war total trade at the Port of Bristol as a whole: between 1914 and 1938 the share of trade handled by the City Docks fell by half, from 55% to 28%.[38] Although the City Docks recovered to some extent from the impact of the war, the river-mouth docks not only recovered but managed to grow pretty consistently throughout the inter-war years. Two measures of the growing dominance of Avonmouth are that by 1939 the City Docks imported only 6,500 tons of grain compared with a massive 985,000 tons entering via Avonmouth. And tobacco imports to the City Docks fell both absolutely and proportionally: in 1935 10,800 tons had come to the Floating Harbour (42 per cent of the total) but by 1939 the amount was only 5,400 tons (11.6 per cent).[39] In this period sugar imports comfortably exceeded tobacco, but in a sure sign of the diminished status of the Floating Harbour, most of it came from coastal traffic. Second, the absolute level of trade in the Floating Harbour remained remarkably constant, given the ups and downs of the wider economy in the period. In most years the total of imports and exports was around 1.2 million tons, with a slight dip to just below 1 million in the slack years of the early 1930s. Equally, there was not much sign of national economic recovery in the later 1930s having any impact on trade in the Harbour.

The Infrastructure

At the beginning of the twentieth century the Port of London faced a crisis, for much of its infrastructure was almost a century old.[40] Was the same true of Bristol's Floating Harbour at the time of its centenary? We have shown in chapter 5 how the authorities had spent heavily on modernising the facilities in the previous 40 years, building new locks at Cumberland Basin, extending the length of quay space, increasing the number of transit sheds and encouraging the GWR to build a rail link to Canon's Marsh. This evidence might lead to the conclusion that the Floating Harbour was a thoroughly modern port, albeit limited to small vessels, of which there were still a very large number. Although it is often assumed that increasing size of ships threatened the viability

Broad Quay in the 1870s. No1 shed (later Dublin shed) was built in 1861 and demolished in 1937. (P 2316)

Broad Quay, May 1937, shortly before work began to cover this stretch of water. (PBA 678)

of places like the Bristol City Docks it remained the case that as late as 1913 the average size of coasters entering the Harbour was only 106 tons.[41] However, in 1924 a report on ports in the UK as a whole was scathing in its criticism of the City Docks:

These docks on the whole are antiquated and inadequately equipped for present-day requirements…All the sheds on the Welsh Back, Grove and Bathurst Wharf, with the exception of the one on the Grove [sic], are quite out of date and in bad order, making it very expensive for steamers to work there.[42]

This report was produced for the Chamber of Shipping and so it may be suspected of special pleading on behalf of shipping interests. For example, it argued that the coasting trade using Bristol had been severely hit by competition and was 'very desirous of securing up-to-date facilities and reduced charges as are provided at certain other ports for coastwise tonnage'.[43] This repeats the age-old call by ship owners who have always wanted expensive modern facilities provided for their use at someone else's expense. The report also specifically called for something that the Docks Committee had been discussing for years, namely the improvement of the quay, provision of deep water berths and railway connection for the timber yards on the south side of the Floating Harbour.

The war delayed a number of capital projects in and around the Floating Harbour, including the construction of the third large bonded warehouse for Imperial Tobacco on the site of the former Clift House, to the south of the New Cut. Work started in February 1915, but there were delays due to shortages of men and materials.[44] At the same time it was noted that the builder, Cowlins, was also involved in a similar project at Canon's Marsh, although this was not completed until 1922.[45] Another scheme that had its first airing in 1915 was the proposed new bridge across the Floating Harbour – at that time there was only Prince Street Bridge between Cumberland Basin and Bristol Bridge.[46] Different locations were considered, at various times, for a crossing between Welsh Back and Redcliffe, but the bridge was not completed until 1942.

One interesting development just after the war was the Committee's agreement to a request by a firm of timber importers to be allowed to move their operations to Cumberland Basin, where there was rail access and much better cargo handling facilities.[47] This is of note because of course the Basin was not intended for loading and unloading (although it had always taken place to some extent, often to lighten ships before entering the Harbour itself). There is evidence that the timber operation continued there for many years.

Work to improve the transit shed facilities was already underway when the report of 1924 was compiled; three sheds at Dean's Marsh, known as T, U and V sheds, which had been built in 1890, were reconstructed by 1927 as two-storey sheds with flat roofs and equipped with modern machinery for goods handling. This was presented as 'the first portion of a comprehensive scheme to be carried out in successive stages for the extension and improvement of the quay and shed facilities at the City Docks to meet modern requirements'.[48] Two further sheds on the Grove were also rebuilt at the same time.[49] However, nothing was ever done to implement the improvements at Baltic Wharf that had been recognised as necessary years before.

As early as 1927 the Docks Committee was asked to consider a report calling for the covering of a further section of St Augustine's Reach, downstream as far as the north end of E shed.[50] It was recognised that this proposal required the provision of extra quay space elsewhere, and Baltic Wharf was mentioned but the preferred option was to develop more of Canon's Marsh, beyond the existing Y and Z sheds. It was not until 1938 that the further portion of St Augustine's Reach was covered, and at the same time work was in hand to build a new wharf and two-storey shed at Fry's Wharf, Canon's Marsh.[51] Meanwhile, the Dublin Shed on Broad Quay (the oldest shed on the Floating Harbour) was demolished as a consequence of covering more of St Augustine's Reach.

1. Jackson, 1983, chapter 6

2. BRO, M/BCC/DOC/1/10, Reports of Officers for 1914, vol 1.

3. Neale, 1976: 3

4. S Palmer, 2000:137

5. Neale, 1970: 22

6. Whitfield, 1983:71

7. Bullock, 1960: 29

8. ibid, p16

9. Whitfield, 1983: 77

10. Bullock, 1960: 41

11. Whyte, 1934: 69

12. Bullock, 1960: 119

13. Whyte, 1934: 67

14. Neale, 1970: 178

15. Whyte, 1934: 59

16. Neale, 1970: 183

17. Bullock, 1960: 25

18. quoted by Neale, 1976, p 65

19. Port of Bristol Official Handbook, 1913, p10

20. P Elkin: 2000, p 26

21. BRO, M/BCC/DOC/1/25, Docks Committee Reports of Officers for 1919, vol 1, Annual Report for the Year to 30 April 1919, p6

22. ibid, p7

23. Neale, 1976, p280

24. BRO, M/BCC/DOC/1/48, Annual Report of the General Manager and Secretary for the year to 31 March 1927, p9

25. Neale, 1970, p5

26. Kelly, 2001: 161-2

27. ibid: 108

28. ibid:1

29. ibid: 2

30. BRO, M/BCC/DOC/1/41, Docks Committee minutes, 27 July 1925, minute 8422

31. Kelly, 2001: 1

32. ibid, p87

33. BRO, M/BCC/DOC/1/43, Annual Report for 1925, p6

34. BRO, M/BCC/DOC/1/10, Reports by Officers, 1914, p404

35. BRO, BCC/M/DOC/1/13, Annual Report for 1915, table 4

36. Kelly, 2001, p215

37. Jackson, 1983, p141

38. figures in this paragraph are calculated from various Annual Reports to the Docks Committee.

39. BRO, M/BCC/DOC/1/80, Reports of Officers for 1939, Annual Report

40. J White: 2008: 172

41. Neale, 1976, p 41. It is also worth noting that the average size of ships entering Avonmouth in 1925 was only 3,800 tons, hardly evidence of a headlong rush to large ships, Annual Report to the Docks Committee, 1925, BRO, M/BCC/DOC/1/43

42. *Port Facilities in Great Britain*, report by the port facilities committee of the Chamber of Shipping of the UK, 1924, p90

43. ibid, p91

44. BRO, M/BCC/DOC/1/13, Reports of Officers for 1915, vol 1, p 735

45. P Jones, 1989

46. BRO, BCC/M/DOC/1/13, Reports of Officers for 1915, vol. 1, 777

47. BRO, BCC/M/DOC/1/24, Reports of Officers for 1919, vol. 1, 16 June 1919.

48. BRO, BCC/M/DOC/1/36, Reports of Officers for 1923, vol. 1, p45

49. BRO, BCC/M/DOC/1/48, Reports of Officers, vol. II, 1927, Annual Report

50. ibid, 14 November 1927

51. BRO, BCC/M/DOC/1/77, Annual Report for 1938

In 1965 the City Docks handled over 1.2 million tons of cargo, the same as in 1939, but within a year or two there was talk of closure. By 1975 commercial activity had virtually ceased, and the long process of reinventing the Floating Harbour had begun. For the best part of a thousand years Bristol had been developing port facilities on the rivers Avon and Frome but now the city authorities faced the challenge of a complete change of direction. How had this state of affairs come about?

One way of looking at the history of the Floating Harbour is to say that once Avonmouth became established, and especially after the completion of the Royal Edward Dock in 1908 and its extension in 1928, it was only a matter of time before shippers abandoned the City Docks, saving themselves the trouble of the hazardous seven-mile journey up river. The growth of road transport continued to undermine the coastal traffic that had been so important to the City Docks, and the connection of Avonmouth to the national motorway system further weakened the position of the old city-centre docks. According to this view, the survival of the Floating Harbour as a working dock into the 1970s was more remarkable than its ultimate demise. But this is to apply the wisdom of hindsight, and it is clear that throughout the 1940s and '50s the Docks Committee continued to see the future of the Harbour in terms of further investment and

Early postwar view of Bristol Bridge from Welsh Back with the isolated remains of Bridge Street and the ruins of St Peter's church beyond. (POS 149)

Ruins of the Corporation Granary after the air raid of 3-4 January 1941. (D 1400)

development, not closure. This was largely because…even in the mid-1950s port towns and cities continued to display many of the physical, social and economic features evident at the beginning of the century. There had been no technological revolution in shipping similar to the nineteenth-century transition from sail to steam which would have had an effect of forcing change in the siting or nature of port facilities. On the quayside, cargo handling continued to be a predominantly manual process, though fork-lift trucks now supplemented cranes as mechanical aids to labour. Within little over a decade all was to change. Containerisation and new modes of discharging high-volume bulk cargoes would rapidly render much of existing port provision, together with its associated workforce, redundant. In this late-twentieth-century world of maritime transport, the connection between city and port was finally severed – only to be rediscovered, or reinvented, as an aspect of urban heritage.'[1]

What happened in the City Docks was being repeated in ports all round the country, and indeed further afield. Of course, in one sense the story of the Floating Harbour in the years from 1939 to 1975 is unique but, as we have seen in earlier periods, the direction of change was driven by external forces beyond the power of local decision makers to resist.

The Docks in Wartime

Much has been written about Bristol during the Second World War,[2] but relatively little attention has been given to the impact on the Docks. The Second World War was quite different from the First in terms of its impact on Bristol and the City Docks. In the Second War the economy was more thoroughly controlled and directed towards the war effort. This meant, for example, that the Ministry of Transport formally assumed control of the principal ports, including Bristol, working through a Port Emergency Committee which was accountable to the Regional Ports Director.[3] The Emergency Committee had wide executive powers to make sure the port continued to work efficiently,

Proctor Baker's (by now Spiller's) granary and mill, Redcliffe Back, with a bombsite to the right. (PBA X2337)

although in practice day-to-day management was left with the port authorities.[4] However, leases on at least three quayside sheds in the Floating Harbour were suspended at the request of the Emergency Committee to ensure adequate storage space for war purposes.[5] Control extended to the principal imports and all British-owned vessels. As a result some liner services trading to Bristol were suspended, including several operated by American-owned vessels which were prohibited by the US government from trading in combatant waters.[6]

Another difference between the two wars was that in 1914-18 trade declined in the Port of Bristol as a whole, whereas in 1939-45 the total volume of trade increased significantly, from five million tons in 1939 to 8.9 million in 1945.[7] However, within these overall figures trade in the City Docks declined by 40 per cent while the port as a whole was increasing by nearly 80 per cent. Nevertheless the First World War precipitated an even greater decline in trade through the City Docks, and can be seen as the key event in the long-term demise.

Finally, although in 1914-18 few people were spared the loss of a close friend or relative in combat, in 1939-45 civilians were themselves directly exposed to the risk of death or injury to an extent unprecedented in the history of warfare, and in the first half of the war civilian casualties exceeded military ones. People living in Bristol were in the front line once the enemy began strategic bombing in the summer of 1940 in an attempt to cripple Britain's economy by attacking its crucial west coast ports.

Accounts of the bombing of Bristol generally dwell on the devastation of the central shopping area of Castle Street, Bridge Street, Wine Street and Mary-le-Port Street, plus considerable damage inflicted to the Victoria Street area on the other side of Bristol Bridge. But these air raids were intended to hit the docks and other strategic targets such as Temple Meads railway station and the nearby goods yards.[8] The damage to homes and businesses across the Bristol area was severe (more than 1,200 people died, over 5,000 homes were destroyed or seriously damaged and 40 acres of the central area were ruined)[9] but it was overwhelmingly due to the lack of precision and inaccuracy of bombing at that time. Bristol was the fourth most heavily bombed city in the country (after London, Liverpool and Birmingham)[10] but the docks escaped largely intact. It is ironic that damage to the City Docks was greater than at Avonmouth, where much more cargo was being moved. A report to the Docks Committee in May 1945 concluded that,

> In spite…of the inconvenience caused, the work of discharging and loading vessels was carried out without interruption and there were relatively few mishaps considering the many risks inseparable from war-time operations.[11]

The first major raid on Bristol came on 24 November 1940, targeting the City Docks, with, according to Penny, 'the intention of eliminating Bristol as an important port supplying much of the Midlands and South of England'.[12] This was when much damage was inflicted on the old shopping area, much more damage than was done to the harbour itself. The bombers returned on the nights of 2 and 6 December to try to finish the job, and on the second of these raids the historic Merchants' Hall near Broad Quay was destroyed. Charles Hill's shipyard was hit and part of the quayside wall on Welsh Back collapsed into the water. Further serious damage was inflicted in central Bristol and locations around the docks, including Bridge Street, High Street, Queen Square, Welsh Back and Broad Quay, on the night of 3-4 January 1941. During this raid the huge Corporation Granary on Prince's Wharf was destroyed, removing an important landscape feature but one that was virtually economically obsolete following the departure of most of the grain trade to Avonmouth in the 1930s. The last serious attack was the Good Friday raid on 11 April 1941, when again docks targets including Canon's Marsh and Broad Quay were hit.

The official report of May 1945 recorded that in addition to the granary the City Docks lost seven transit sheds plus six that were badly damaged.[13] Bombs destroyed some buildings at Underfall Yard and damaged the culverts between the harbour and the river. In the same raid a privately-owned former flour mill on Redcliffe Back was hit. Damage was widespread, from Cumberland Basin in the west through to St Philip's Bridge in the east. The destruction of this bridge not only disrupted road traffic but also severed the power cables for the trams (thereby putting the final nail in the coffin of Bristol's tramway system) and blocked the passage of barges using the Floating Harbour upstream from Bristol Bridge.

The City Docks remained operational throughout the war, despite the bombing (which was effectively confined to less than six months out of a war lasting nearly six years). As a precaution against the danger of bombing leading to a catastrophic draining of the entire Floating Harbour the two minor sets of access locks at Bathust Basin and at Totterdown were blocked off by rubble (which was never removed). Although Cumberland Basin was hit and the Underfall was damaged the Docks escaped the nightmare of a complete loss of

Newly-built L and M sheds, Prince's Wharf, 1952. (PBA1972)

water. In some cases damaged buildings were merely cleared away so that the sites could be used as open quays, while in other cases scarce resources were found to carry out repairs and reinstatement. The Waterford shed at Cumberland Basin was cleared away, as were the remains of the Corporation Granary and the sheds nearby that suffered in the same raid; two damaged sheds on the Grove were also removed. But in December 1941 it was decided to spend a total of £25,000 repairing W, U and E sheds on Dean's Marsh.[14]

As in the First World War, the conflict generated increased work for Charles Hill's shipyard on the Floating Harbour, which was kept busy with orders from the Navy, despite being hit by at least two bombs.[15] According to the Docks Committee report on wartime activities, some 28 ships were launched.[16] The cleared site of the Corporation granary and transit sheds on Princes Wharf became the base for a landing craft unit from 1943. Over 1,000 small landing craft and harbour service vessels arrived here by road and were unloaded by the Fairbairn steam crane. They were then prepared for tropical service in makeshift

Docks Committee meeting at Queen Square 27 May 1957. (PBA N1061)

workshops on the site before being craned into the docks and driven down the river to waiting troop ships off Portishead.

The demands of the war effort brought changes in the workings of the docks. For instance, it became even more important to load and unload ships as quickly as possible, to minimise the exposure of valuable cargoes to the dangers of known target areas. Ships which had previously visited Bristol to offload just a part of a cargo would now be emptied completely. From the dockers' point of view the war created additional risk and danger, not only in terms of air raids but also working in the hours of darkness under blackout conditions. On the other hand there was always plenty of work to do, and overtime to be earned; the normal working day was extended to twelve and a half hours, plus weekends. The demand for dock labour in the Port of Bristol as a whole was such that workers were brought in from other ports and military personnel were also deployed. As in many other areas of life wartime conditions proved a catalyst for change, and the essential nature of dock work led to measures that gave dockers greater security of employment. Emergency powers legislation enabled the former Bristol dockers' union organiser, Ernest Bevin (now Minister of Labour in Churchill's wartime coalition government), to introduce job security for registered dockers. At the end of 1941 Bristol was one of the first ports to benefit from Bevin's initiative.

The Port Emergency Committee consisted of 'representatives of the Port authority, of shipping, road, rail and canal interests, various Ministries, traders, organised labour, the British fighting services and later the Americans'.[17] The Docks Committee itself continued to be chaired by Alderman Burgess throughout the war, and Mr R H Jones remained in post as the general manager until his retirement in September 1945, after 52 years' service.[18] There was, therefore, considerable experience and continuity during a very challenging time. Also throughout the war the city council was evenly balanced between Labour and Citizen Party members. For the first time since the construction of the Floating Harbour councillors were not required to ask ratepayers to make a financial contribution towards meeting its costs.

Post-war Reconstruction

Bristol emerged from the war as a very different place, with large areas of the inner city destroyed or seriously damaged. However, plans for reconstruction were already under discussion as early as 1941, and the wartime devastation can be seen as both delaying and giving a boost to ideas that had been around since the 1930s.[19] The Floating Harbour had already been affected by two schemes designed to improve traffic flows around the inner area: the late-1930s culverting of more of St Augustine's Reach and the construction of Redcliffe Bridge. The devastated shopping area became the centre of attention and much controversy raged around the proposal to re-locate it to Broadmead.[20] Ambitious proposals were put forward for radical rebuilding of large parts of the city centre, well beyond the most seriously damaged areas, but all seeming to assume that the docks would carry on as before.[21] Nevertheless, the remodelling proposal put by the City Council to the Minister in 1944 embraced a significant part of the Floating Harbour (east of the western end of Wapping Wharf and the old gas works on the Canon's Marsh side) within an area in which the council sought compulsory purchase powers pending comprehensive redevelopment.[22] This was rejected and a much smaller area was finally approved, in 1948; now the Floating Harbour was excluded except for the Redcliffe side upstream from Bathurst Basin on the left bank and upstream from the King Street-Welsh Back junction on the right bank. In other words the most economically active parts of the harbour were excluded from the plan, and the Redcliffe Back buildings that were included were largely abandoned flour mills or bombed sites.

An important aspect of post-war planning in general, and in Bristol in particular, was the emphasis on zoning, quite large areas in which specific land uses would predominate. In the case of the City Docks the plans simply accepted the existing land uses, presumably on the grounds that docks, unlike, say, shopping areas, cannot be relocated.[23] Writers such as Michael Jenner and John Punter[24] have

Discharging woodpulp at Welsh Back, May 1950, with evidence of bomb damage to the right. (PBA 1896)

criticised the decisions made during the post-war redevelopment of Bristol, not least the way in which the planners over-estimated the resources that would be available.

While the City Docks were excluded from the grandiose schemes for post-war reconstruction it is important to recognise that this may have worked to their advantage, if only because it meant the Docks Committee was free to continue without the inertia imposed by a grand but unrealisable plan. In the context of the time – characterised by an emphasis on eliminating inappropriate land uses and a tolerance (tending towards enthusiasm) for demolishing buildings of historic importance – it is perhaps surprising that the Floating Harbour was not condemned as obsolete and anachronistic. By the end of the war the City Docks were handling little more than a third as much freight as in 1914, and, as we have seen, there was bomb damage that might have supported the argument that the Docks had no future. No-one made that argument until much later, and in the meantime it was business as usual.

Unloading African hardwood logs at Broad Quay, May 1956. (PBA B895)

The story of the Floating Harbour in the first 20 years after the Second World War is one of sustained recovery, growth and investment. Only after 1965 was there a decline in trade and an end to new investment.

An early sign of the optimism of the Docks Committee about the prospects for the City Docks was the decision in July 1945 to buy the WCA Warehouse on Redcliffe Back.[25] The adjacent Spiller's warehouses and mills had been purchased in 1932 and the WCA Warehouse would give the Committee a water frontage of some 200 yards, and 'It has been agreed…that its future development should be for the provision of waterside warehouses making suitable use of Port facilities'. The following year's Annual Report noted that, '…plans have been approved for two new Transit Sheds, Prince's Wharf, and the provision of new facilities and accommodation at Bathurst Wharf…In conjunction with the Planning and Reconstruction Committee new layouts have been agreed upon for the Welsh Back, timber Wharves at Cumberland Road and waterside premises between Cumberland Basin and Temple Meads'.[26] Some of the planned investment was about rebuilding war-damaged sheds. Thus, for example, L and M sheds on Prince's Wharf (in 2009 being redeveloped into the Museum of Bristol) were completed by 1952 (having been delayed by shortages of materials).

The project at Bathurst Wharf concerned the decision to invest £55,000 to provide modified sheds and offices for the Bristol Steam Navigation Company, which had expressed its desire to restart its regular service to Rotterdam and Antwerp. The company's argument was that in order to do so successfully it needed a guaranteed berth with improved cranes and rail connections. In return for the Docks Committee's investment the company agreed to take a 21-year lease.[27] This was an early post-war example of a growing and much wider trend towards shipping companies demanding dedicated berths and improved handling facilities. In 1955 the Docks Committee agreed to build a warehouse at Prince's Wharf for the exclusive use of the Guinness company.[28]

Fairbairn steam crane (1876) coping with new container technology in 1970. (P 14133)

Another indication of the Committee's optimistic view of the future was that in May 1950 they reviewed a number of sites around the Floating Harbour, making recommendations as to how these should be identified under planning legislation. The Committee saw the Canon's Marsh gas works site as one that they would like to acquire for provision of extended quayside and further shed accommodation (with good rail access), even though the gas works was not expected to close within ten years. A number of other sites were also identified as having potential for the extension of port activities.[29]

Trade within the City Docks increased by nearly 40 per cent between 1946 and 1948. It then fell back again before a more sustained increase until 1956, although this peak, of almost 1.1 million tons was still only equivalent to the average levels achieved between the wars, and only half of the 1914 all-time record. So although there was certainly plenty of activity at the City quays (more than 3,000 vessels entered the Floating Harbour in 1956), the impression of busy-ness was perhaps enhanced by comparison with the more recent past. The overwhelming proportion of trade was coastal imports, continuing,

New Stothert & Pitt cranes on Wapping Wharf in 1965. In 1972 they were moved to Portishead. (D 9276)

indeed reinforcing, a longstanding pattern. Timber continued to be a significant import, reflecting the requirements of the house-building boom in the 1950s, but grain imports to the City Docks had dwindled to nothing. Writing about this period Elkin says that, 'A large part of the south and west of England in general still looked to Bristol for commercial and shipping services and coastal shipping operators continued to provide weekly services between the City Docks and other major ports including London, Liverpool, Hull, Glasgow and Southampton'.[30]

Following a short period of falling trade in the late 1950s activity picked up again and climbed to a post-war peak of 1.25 million tons in 1965. This buoyancy may have encouraged the Docks Committee to press ahead with further investment. In 1964 the City Council bought a strip of land along the length of Wapping Railway Wharf from British Railways in order to improve and modernise facilities there. Three new rail tracks were laid down and a number of new cranes were provided for the Baltic timber trade.[31] However, despite the high level of trade achieved in the mid-1960s the signs were ominous. It was also in 1960 that the City Council submitted its first scheme to develop what was then referred to as the West Dock (now Royal Portbury) on the west bank of the river at Avonmouth.[32] The fact that the City pressed ahead with this major investment, despite refusal of government financial support, had the effect of starving the City Docks of any further investment.[33]

In 1965 the Canon's Marsh goods yard closed, another sign of changing times. Other closures also had implications for shipping activity in the Docks: for instance, the closure of the town gas works at Canon's Marsh and at Avon Street in the mid-1960s immediately meant no further need for coal deliveries and coke collection by ship. This had a knock-on effect for Butler's tar works, which had nowhere to collect coal tar any longer. Similarly, all along Avon Street and Cheese Lane and the Feeder Canal were heavy industries traditionally supplied by water – lead works, galvanising works, Distillers yeast factory, Netham alkali works – all encouraged by zoning to remove

Morris Minors lined up for export in December 1949 in front of Neptune and the CWS building on Narrow Quay. (PBA 1478)

themselves, mostly to Avonmouth. Railway closure at Canon's Marsh and at Wapping Wharf in 1965 was driven by British Railways after the Beeching Report and removed a significant transport infrastructure, further reducing the City Docks' flexibility. Other changes at this time included the closure of the extensive Lysaght engineering works on the Feeder Canal and the coal importing operation at Poole's Wharf.

Towards Closure

Containerisation was about to have a devastating impact on old-established ports everywhere, not least great ports such as London and Liverpool. The transformation due to containerisation was far more rapid than the nineteenth-century transition to steam power, and in the case of Liverpool its impact has been described as 'brutal'.[34] In London the great docks that were built at about the same time as the Floating Harbour began to close in the late 1960s, but as Stephen Inwood has pointed out it was not a decline in trade but rather an expansion that killed off these old docks.[35] Containerisation was supplemented by two other key innovations, palletisation and roll-on-roll-off ships. These enabled cargo-carrying ships to become very much larger and required specialised new loading facilities and dedicated berths. Mechanisation of bulk cargoes such as coal and grain had been achieved in the nineteenth century, but according to Gordon Jackson, 'The miscellaneous trades could rely on no such devices. Most goods still, in 1945, came or went in 'man-sized' boxes, barrels and packages that were stacked loose in sheds, on quays and in holds, and trundled endlessly around'.[36] It was almost physically impossible to unload very large ships using these traditional techniques, at least within economically viable timescales. Palletisation, roll-on-roll-off and containerisation provided ways of moving much larger quantities of non-bulk items, allowing ships to be built to grander dimensions, and killing off small ports that were ill-equipped to receive them.

From the ship owners' point of view the container revolution had the added advantage of enabling them to reduce or even eliminate

Unloading Irish butter July 1963. This image graphically conveys the huge amount of manual work required to load and unload general cargo vessels before containers. (PBA N3664)

the use of traditional dock labour, and it was perhaps not entirely coincidental that containerisation developed at the same time as decasualisation was finally achieved, in 1967.

As far as the Floating Harbour was concerned, its fate was probably sealed by a combination of factors, including its up-stream location, the growth of road traffic and an extended motorway system. The world-wide revolution in shipping was just the last straw, but it is worth recording that as late as 1970 the City Docks were still handling very nearly 800,000 tons of cargo, albeit only a little more than 10 per cent of the Bristol total.[37] In that sense there was still clearly a role for the old harbour, but what really strengthened the hand of those arguing for closure was the rising losses sustained on the City Docks part of the port of Bristol. In 1971 the loss was recorded at £297,000, and by its final year of trading, the year to March 1975, the loss had mounted to £359,000.[38]

1. S Palmer, 'Ports' in M Daunton (ed) *Cambridge Urban History of Britain*, vol III, p150
2. C M MacInnes, *Bristol at War*, 1962, J Penny, *Bristol at War*, Breedon Books, 2002, H Reid, *Bristol Under Siege*, Redcliffe Press, 2005, J Hasegawa, *Replanning the Blitzed City Centre*, Open University Press, 1992
3. MacInnes, op cit: 186
4. Port of Bristol Authority Annual Report for the year to 31 March 1940, p 6, BRO, M/BCC/DOC/1/83
5. Minutes of the Docks Committee, 13 January 1941, BRO, BCC/M/DOC/1/86
6. ibid, p6
7. Port of Bristol Authority Annual Report for the year to 31 March 1946, BRO, M/BCC/DOC/1/95
8. Reid, 2005: 14
9. Penny, 1995, Hasegawa, 1992
10. ibid, p1.
11. BRO, M/BCC/DOC/1/93, 'Wartime Activities of the Port', May 1945, p3
12. Penny, 1995:8
13. BRO, M/BCC/DOC/1/93, 'Wartime Activities of the Port', May 1945, p3
14. BRO, M/BCC/DOC/1/86, Minutes of the Docks Committee for 1941, 22 December.
15. Wall and Shipsides, 1981: 121
16. BRO, M/BCC/DOC/1/93, May 1945 p3
17. MacInnes, 1962:186
18. BRO, M/BCC/DOC/1/95, Annual Report for the year to 31 March 1946
19. for fuller accounts see Hasegawa, 1992 and J Punter, *Design Control in Bristol, 1940-1990*, Redcliffe Press, 1990.
20. M Jenner, in *Post-war Bristol 1945-65*, Bristol Branch of the Historical Association, 2000
21. eg, *English City*, 1945
22. Punter, 1990: 32
23. ibid, p42
24. Jenner, op cit, and Punter op cit
25. BRO, M/BCC/DOC/1/113, Reports of Officers for 1945, 23 July.
26. BRO, M/BCC/DOC/1/95, Annual Report for 1946, pp7-8
27. BRO, M/BCC/DOC/1/95, 18 March 1946.
28. BRO, M/BCC/DOC/1/113, report dated 24 February 1955
29. BRO, M/BCC/DOC/1/103, Reports of Officers for 1950, report dated 8 May 1950.
30. Elkin, op cit: 29
31. ibid, p44
32. K Bassett, and A Hoare, 'Bristol and the saga of Royal Portbury: a case study in local politics and municipal enterprise' *Political Geography Quarterly*, vol. 3, no. 3, July 1984, pp223-250
33. Elkin, op cit, p 44
34. G Milne, in Belcham, 2006, p264
35. S Inwood, *A History of London*, 1998: 900
36. Jackson, 1983: 152
37. Annual Report for 1970
38. Annual Report for 1975

On 15 December 1969, over 1,200 people packed the Colston Hall for a Town Meeting, called to debate proposals to close the City Docks to commercial traffic. At the end of the meeting, a vote was called; of the 724 ratepayers eligible to vote, 560 opposed the Council's plans for closure. The victory here has been seen as a triumph for the conservation lobby and the start of an effective opposition to what were seen as increasingly philistine Council planning policies. The true picture, as ever, is much more complicated.

The Council's Local Plan issued in 1966[1] hardly mentioned the City Docks. The Port was still seen as a permanent part of the city's character, and there was little sense of the immense changes that were about to hit the shipping world. Although in the previous year the Bristol Steam Navigation Co had equipped Princes Wharf with a 25-ton capacity crane to handle containers on their twice-weekly Dublin service, and had decided to convert two vessels solely to carry them, the wholesale and speedy changeover to 'boxes' by most shipping lines was not expected to have much effect on the Floating Harbour's

traffic. This, after all, was primarily made up of continental and coastal trade, small vessels from Rotterdam or Scandinavia. By the end of the decade, almost all this trade was being brought in containers to east coast ports and across country by road. In June 1963, 80 ships berthed in the City Docks; in October 1969, only 28 called.[2]

There had long been plans for an expansion of the river-mouth docks, this time on the western side of the river Avon. Almost since the end of World War II, the City Council had quietly been purchasing land around Portbury and in 1960 initial proposals for a new dock were presented to Parliament. The government sent the plans back, commenting that the scale was far too big. The PBA revised the scheme and modified its design from traditional break-bulk wharves and sheds to a much simpler single basin designed with the increasing size of container and bulk vessels in mind. Nevertheless, the revised scheme was still turned down; Sir Robert Wall attributes this to the opposition of the Welsh MPs, fearful of the adverse effect that a new dock would have on the trade of Newport, Barry and Cardiff.[3] For

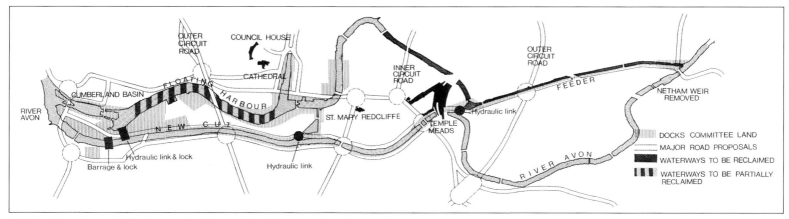

The *Civic News* August 1969 plan to 'reclaim' parts of the Floating Harbour. (D 10423)

Large crowds turned out to welcome home the *Great Britain* in July 1970. (GB 3)

whatever reason, the West Dock scheme finally gained approval from the Heath government in 1970 (provided that Bristol funded it with no help from government). Work began in 1972 and the new dock, renamed Royal Portbury, was opened by the Queen in 1977; its eventual success in the 1990s is what has kept Bristol in the forefront of the shipping industry in the 21st century, but that is another story.

Plans for Closure

Confident of the likely approval of the West Dock in 1969, the Port's management began to make plans for the closure of the City Docks. Considerable thought was given to the later role of the Floating Harbour. Some urgency was necessary; it was widely believed at the time that the Labour government's Docks Nationalisation Bill would include Bristol and would potentially strip the City of any land that was still considered operational. Although this never occurred, it is another factor in the unusual speed with which matters progressed.

Some public indications of impending closure started to appear in September 1968, when the *Evening Post* ran a series of articles un-der the headline 'If The Ships Go'.[4] These were written by the Bristol Planning Group, members of the City's Planning and Transport Departments, and addressed all the points of contention that would later emerge. The chief two were the apparent obsession with providing new roads and, to achieve this, the potential for filling in or covering large areas of the docks. The articles ranged widely, considering the potential of using the drained Harbour bed for roads (not feasible) or for a short rail link from Temple Meads to St Philips Bridge (some potential for reducing city centre car parking). They concluded that there was little benefit in reclaiming much of the land, but nevertheless some reduction was worthwhile.

There are thus some grounds for believing the politicians from both Labour and Conservative groups who have consistently maintained that there was never any likelihood of the controversial scheme that appeared in the *Civic News* of August 1969.[5] Always blamed on officer sabotage, the appearance of a plan involving large-scale infilling was bound to provoke outcry. The scheme was predicated upon damming the Avon New Cut close to the Underfall Yard, making the Cut and the river non-tidal and removing the need for Netham Weir. This would create a 'cruiseway' of sufficient dimensions to allow pleasure craft to navigate it, and access to the rest of the Harbour would be created or reopened at the now-redundant Underfall Dam, Bathurst Basin and Totterdown Locks. The Feeder Canal, at this time in very poor repair, would be closed and filled, together with the stretch of the Harbour from Totterdown Lock to St Philips Bridge. Most controversial of all, the Harbour between the bottom of St Augustine's Reach and Baltic Wharf would be mostly reclaimed, retaining a narrow channel and a series of lagoons to help the Harbour to maintain its role in drainage and flood defence. Larger vessels would still be able to visit at Cumberland Basin, but would be unable to proceed further.

The resulting public outcry led to the public meeting at the Colston Hall where a loose alliance of conservation and amenity groups joined with water sports and boating interests to force a Town Poll on the City Council. Claiming throughout that filling the Docks

Launch of the last ship to be built in Bristol, the *Miranda Guinness*, 9 July 1976. (BIM slide 802)

had never been their intention, councillors and officers vainly argued their case. Councillor Bell claimed, 'We put forward the *Civic News* in order to generate public discussion. We have made one or two errors in this'.[6]

The opponents of the apparent plan couldn't have agreed more. Their fears (for which there was much justification) were that the closure proposals were solely for the benefit of the road lobby. Already, plans for the new Inner Ring Road showed a major dual carriageway launching itself from Redcliffe Bridge across St Augustine's Reach, demolishing the group of Georgian buildings on Prince Street that included the Shakespeare pub, before cutting through Canon's Marsh to join a major junction with the proposed Outer Ring Road, at the bottom of Jacobs Wells Road. In anticipation of this major new route, the Unicorn (now Jury's) hotel with adjacent multi-deck car parking had already established itself on adjoining land on Prince Street. The *Civic News* article pointed out that the bridge over the Reach could be a lot lower without the shipping to contend with.

Faced with such organised and vocal opposition, the Council launched an effective campaign to mobilise a vote in its favour, and the Town Poll returned a considerable majority (22,298 against 16,724) supporting the Council's plans. Later all but one Councillor voted for the plan and the Bristol Corporation Bill was duly sent to Parliament and enacted in 1971. It contained within it all of the powers requested by the members for closing and reclaiming parts of the Harbour, in particular Temple Back and the Feeder Canal.

In July 1970, the *Great Britain* returned to Bristol. The astounding adventure of her salvage from the Falkland Islands had aroused enormous public interest by the time she reached Avonmouth, so that crowds of over 200,000 lined the Avon to see the final leg of her journey. This unprecedented enthusiasm for a piece of Britain's, and Bristol's, industrial and maritime heritage was the point at which the tide began to turn in favour of conservation, and was to heavily influence the approach taken thereafter to the redevelopment of the Harbour. It was by no means guaranteed, however, and there was even a debate about whether the ship should stay in Bristol. The ship's Trust had to wait until 1975 before the Council finally agreed to her remaining in the Great Western Dock in perpetuity for a peppercorn rent; even then, the continued antipathy of some councillors meant that the adjoining car park and canteen had to pay full commercial rates.[7]

Following the passage of the 1971 Act, the Council appointed Casson Conder & Partners to prepare a conceptual study[8] that would allow phased development of the Harbour. Their report met with general approval from the interest groups that had started to form around the Harbour, with the exception of their proposal for twin 20-storey towers on Princes Wharf. There were some who felt that the balance of office (too much) to industry (not enough) needed redressing. Sir Hugh Casson himself drew attention to the constraints of the many road proposals under consideration, illustrating their impact by overlaying all of them on one map, and commenting particularly on the impact on the *Great Britain* of the proposed Outer Circuit Road bridge oversailing the Harbour close to it. 'The proposals for the Outer Circuit Road crossing the Floating Harbour and the multi-level junction on the south bank should most seriously be reconsidered. [The area] cannot accommodate an Urban motorway of this scale without very great disturbance to its unique character'.[9] Overall the proposals for mixed development with many public amenities, including a marina, maritime museum, swimming pool, sports centre, bus station, car parks, law courts and a major hotel were a model of their kind, common in the early 21st century but quite radical in the early 1970s.

The Casson Report's introduction recommended 'examination of designs for this area – always given the widest publicity in time for public opinion to be heard – should be vigorous and positive. Only the best is good enough here. This does not mean timidity exaggerated into hostility towards anything new. Future conservationists will look, as we do today, for buildings of individuality and character to cherish, and will expect to find some'.[10] A number of factors now came into play to influence future development. Firstly, those who had hitherto opposed the City's plans decided to adopt a positive approach and formed the City Docks Group. The Group, which included some of the most influential architects, engineers, conservationists and individuals in Bristol at the time, prepared and presented a series of seven reports on different aspects of the Harbour, building on Casson's report, between 1974 and 1977. The most influential of them, a study by James Bruges, demonstrated how much more beneficially the land could be used without the road proposals.[11] The Council could not afford to ignore this influential input and, although relations were not always cordial, it set a pattern of consultation that became a model for other cities.

Secondly, politicians and officers changed. The new Labour Council in the early 1970s included a number of younger members who were not tied to the post-war road plans of their predecessors. Then in 1974 the creation of the County of Avon removed responsibility for

Transport and Highways from Bristol, many of the officers associated with the earlier plans moving across to the new authority. There was immediate mistrust between the two authorities, which had the effect of slowing the pace of change. All the chief officers who considered the Casson Report for Bristol City Council in 1974 were new to the authority and had no in-depth knowledge of the pre-1971 work; at the time, they saw this as a disadvantage, delaying the process whilst they tried to get up to speed, but it did allow fresh minds to come to bear.

Finally, and most influentially, there was a spectacular property crash after 1973. Almost all major development in Bristol ceased until 1980, and the number of large-scale planning applications reduced to a trickle, allowing a period of reassessment and reconsideration. This saved Bristol from further office development such as the Bristol & West building that had grown to dominate the Centre and the head

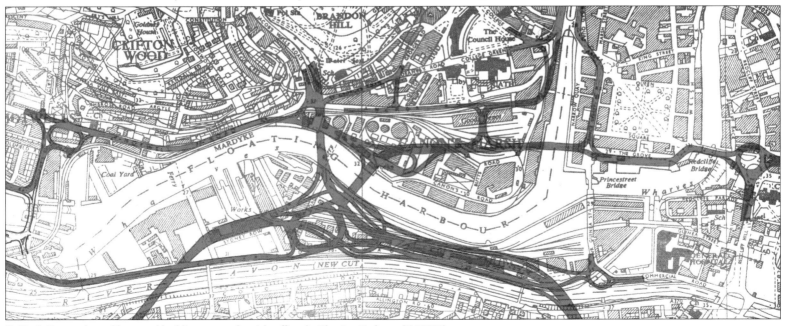

Sir Hugh Casson showed how road building proposals might affect the Floating Harbour. (D 10424)

of St Augustine's Reach, and was imminently due to be joined by a similar structure on the site of the Co-operative Wholesale Society building. The CWS was demolished in 1973, but the office tower, permission for which the Planning Committee felt it had no grounds to deny, was shelved at the start of the slump.

A Survey of the Floating Harbour

The Port of Bristol Authority passed responsibility for the City Docks to the City Council on 1 April 1975. It is worth pausing here to consider what the Harbour looked like at this date. In general, there was an air of dereliction, although this is often the atmosphere that even thriving and active docks impart! At the western extreme, Cumberland Basin continued to operate as the main entrance locks for the dock system, and still served the regular sand traffic and occasional coaster or naval visit that continued to navigate the Avon. The Underfall Yard still functioned as the base for the substantial force of engineers, millwrights, shipwrights and fitters required to maintain the Harbour's infrastructure, but now in the control of the City Engineers Department. Adjacent on Baltic Wharf, the former timber wharfs had ceased to welcome ships some time previously, although the companies continued to store timber there, and one, Robbins, maintained a sawmill. The Albion Dockyard still built ships, although its days were known to be numbered: the 1971 Act had provided for generous compensation for Charles Hill & Sons and they launched their last vessel, the tanker *Miranda Guinness*, in 1976.

On the north bank of the Harbour, the Merchants' Dock had been filled in 1967. Poole's Wharf next door had ceased to act as a coal-importing wharf but continued to handle sand and gravel dredged from the Severn Estuary by Silveys. They would later be joined by the Bristol Sand & Gravel Co and Holms Sand & Gravel as they were displaced from Redcliffe Back and Bathurst Basin. Mardyke had been home to the RNVR on the static drill ship *Flying Fox* until she was scrapped in 1973 when the base had moved ashore, but their seago-

Canon's Marsh before May 1988, when the tobacco bonds were demolished, along with everything else in this picture except the stone crane tower in the foreground and the cathedral in the background. (P 14117)

ing training ship HMS *Venturer* still moored there between trips. Brandon Wharf was in use by a builders' merchants, but the former town gas works at Canon's Marsh had ceased production in the mid-1960s and now served solely as a store for natural gas in its two gasholders. The dereliction here was enhanced by the Gas Board's removal of the roofs from several buildings (to avoid paying rates on them) and the reduction in height of the Harbour-facing administration buildings. The former Canon's Marsh railway marshalling yard and goods shed further east served as a car park, masked from the Harbour by A, Z and Y Sheds, all in short-term occupation for a variety of light industrial uses. The area was dominated by Imperial Tobacco's two 1920s concrete bonded warehouses, then still in use.

On the south bank Wapping Wharf still had railway sidings covering most of its expanse, with coal storage compounds close to the *Great Britain* site. On Princes Wharf, where the last cargo of all had been landed in November 1974, stood four of the original eight electric cranes, the last surviving cargo cranes in the Harbour; we will

The sand dredger *Camerton* passing through Redcliffe bridge in 1972. (Keen 837)

come to their story soon. Behind L and M Sheds, the former railway goods yard thrived as a coal distribution depot run by Lowell Baldwin. On Bathurst Wharf, the transit sheds were disused and derelict in front of the similarly run-down former Robinsons oil seed mill that had served as a bonded store. The Basin continued to be used as a base by the Holms Sand & Gravel Co until 1980. Redcliffe Wharf was a Council building materials yard.

Beyond Redcliffe bridge, the quayside on both banks was a continuous run of underused semi-derelict dockside sheds, mills and granaries; the bridge still rose regularly to allow the passage of Bristol Sand & Gravel's vessels plying to and from their base on Redcliffe Back. Between Bristol Bridge and St Philips Bridge, Courages brewery on the south bank and the green expanse of Castle Park provided temporary relief before a further expanse of industrial wasteland along Temple Back and Avon Street and along the Feeder Canal. The Port had long ago relinquished interest in the upper reaches of the Harbour, however.

The agreement between the PBA and the City required the Authority to clear away any redundant equipment as it vacated its premises. This had resulted in the steady disappearance of dockside machinery, particularly cranes, after 1969. The sole survivor was intended to be the Victorian Fairbairn steam crane, handed to the City Museum in 1973. Faced with the disappearance of the last survivors in 1975, a group called City Docks Ventures (including John Sansom, this book's publisher) was formed specifically to purchase two of the electric cranes on Princes Wharf back from the scrap man. The City's Arts & Leisure Committee stepped in and bought the other two, ensuring the survival of a representative group on the Harbour by the skin of their teeth.

There were signs of positive change, however. The transit sheds on the west side of St Augustine's Reach had found new uses as an Exhibition Centre (U and V Sheds) and as an early home for the Arnolfini art gallery (W Shed). In 1974, Arnolfini announced it would be moving into the Bush warehouse at the end of the Reach, after its

Power-boat racing was a popular but dangerous annual attraction in the Harbour. (D 10425)

conversion into two floors of gallery and the remainder as offices by the JT Group. Its opening in 1975 is widely viewed as a landmark in the regeneration of the Docks, not so much because of the number of visitors it attracted as that 'they tended to be those who formed opinion in the city'.[12] It undoubtedly attracted attention, but other more lowly souls were learning about the potential of the Harbour too. The *Great Britain* attracted significant numbers of people likely to be interested also in their industrial surroundings, and the growing popularity of the annual Bristol Harbour Regatta (first held in 1971 as the Water Festival) and the spectacularly dangerous Powerboat Grand Prix (held annually from 1972 until 1991) served to bring more and more ordinary people to the water. Within a couple of years, these attractions had been joined by Bristol Industrial Museum, which with its attendant steam railway became a major destination for visitors after 1978. City Docks Ventures, having bought the Princes Wharf cranes, turned their attention to establishing a Water Bus service in

1976; this has continued to thrive as the Ferry Boat Co. They joined the Bristol Packet who had operated docks tours in the tradition of the old 'penny steamers' but with admirably opinionated commentaries since 1974 on their narrowboat *Redshank*. Also on the water, the City offered sites for floating restaurants, one of which was taken for the old Caledonian Macbrayne ferry *Lochiel* in 1978. On Welsh Back, the *Lightship* opened around the same time, providing a convenient watering hole for detective Eddie Shoestring in the BBC TV series aired in 1979/80.

Abandoning the 1971 Act

Bristol's chief officers reported back to the Council on their consideration of the Casson Report in April 1975, just after the handover and again in 1976. On both occasions they recommended that the 1971 Act be abandoned, largely because there was no longer time to implement the engineering works outlined in it. Instead, their second report proposed allowing commercial ships (including the sand trade but not Hill's shipbuilding yard) to continue to use the Harbour for the time being, to reconstruct the crumbling Cumberland Basin walls and renew the stop gates and to introduce a cutter-suction dredger to maintain the depth. Alternative proposals for a barrage at Avonmouth, Pill, Horseshoe Bend or Black Rock (ironically where Nickalls had proposed the very first dam to create a Floating Harbour in 1786) which could deliver greater benefits than one near Underfall Yard for little extra cost were considered by Alexander Gibbs & Partners. Despite the positive reasons for adopting one of these, the officers recommended the barrage be abandoned, again because time constraints would make it impossible to achieve under the 1971 Act and preparing a second Bill to obtain the necessary powers would be expensive. The Council officially abandoned the Act in April 1976, bringing to a close a seven-year period of uncertainty.

Despite these small rumblings of change, it was apparent that an enormous effort would be required to revive the Harbour. The draft Local Plan that developed from the Casson Report stated 'the strong ties that once existed between the City and its Port have now been severed, and the use of the City Docks now bears little or no functional relationship to the needs of the city as a whole'.[13] This plan, entitled *The Opportunities of the Docks* built on Casson's Report and on the seven City Docks Group documents to create an overall vision for longer-term development combined with pragmatic thoughts for the short- to medium-term development of the Harbour. It pointed out again that 'influencing many of the possible courses of action are the longstanding commitments to large-scale road proposals which have, possibly more than any other factor, been responsible for the blighting and sterilisation of large tracts of land in the Study Area'.[14] These sentiments, together with the thoughtful approach taken to the whole area, meant that the Plan received universal approval. It was to be another four years before Avon County Council formally abandoned the road schemes, but in effect, they were already long obsolete.

The adoption of so consensual a Local Plan set the course for the next decade. In combination with BALUT (the Bristol Area Land Use & Transportation survey) carried out for Avon County Council, it effectively controlled speculative office development. Its recommendation, that the entire Docks area should be declared a Conservation Area and thereby require every application for development to take the overall heritage of the area into consideration, was adopted immediately and is widely considered to have improved the quality of almost every development since.

Progress was nevertheless painfully slow. The Local Plan aimed for an even balance between public, private and 'fair rent' (i.e housing association) housing development. Land at Baltic Wharf was earmarked for a council housing scheme, but the Thatcher government's hostile attitude towards social housing and its removal of funding from the Housing Corporation put an end to this. A small development over the old Merchants' Dock began in 1980, originally schemed as mixed housing with offices fronting Hotwells Road, but completed wholly as housing. Called Rownham Meads, it began the trend to what one

By late 1990s new housing schemes had been built on the sites of Merchants' Dock, Stothert's Shipyard and the Baltic Wharf timber yards. (PM slide 14)

Bathurst Wharf before its transformation into homes and offices in the 1980s. (Day E1)

observer has referred to as 'aestheticising' traditional names.[15]

It was followed by the development of Bathurst Basin a year later. This site had been the subject of a planning appeal in 1977 when the owners' application for light industrial development had been denied. The Inspector hearing the appeal dismissed it on two grounds – that the docks area should be developed for recreational and cultural benefit and that the specific site was of enormous strategic importance because of its position – giving official backing to the vision of the Local Plan[16]. A mixed housing and office development followed, with key elements of conservation in the cottages and pub at the southern end of the site and the Bristol Byzantine frontages of the former Robinsons seed warehouse and office; sadly, the oil seed mill and transit sheds which might have survived in a later scheme were demolished. Bathurst Wharf became Merchant's Landing and the first phase was complete by 1982.

About the same time, with a political change in the Council to Conservative control, land at Baltic Wharf was marketed for a private housing scheme. The land had been cleared in readiness for development in the late 1970s, and portions allocated to other use: at the western end, a water sports area and caravan park were set up, whilst Charles Hill's former shipyard began to develop into a pleasure craft marina and boat repair space. Between these, a new housing scheme with a private developer but with a social provision to try to achieve low-cost houses was created. The whole development was completed in two years and, to its credit, memorialised the old wharf names of Canada, Gefle and Cumberland in its street plan. A subsidised purchase scheme attracted first-time buyers, but the rapidly rising prices of housing at this period soon made the new units unaffordable to many. A planning requirement that the developers should provide an element of public art, via a sculpture competition, produced three waterfront sculptures by leading artists, including Bristol-born Stephen Cox.

As property prices continued to rise, the City Council sought to ensure that more homes were available to the less-well-off. Two housing associations had put forward schemes for refurbishing Proctor Baker's mill and granary (by now known as Buchanan's Wharf) on Redcliffe Back in 1979 but the government's attitude to public housing had

Z shed, Canon's Marsh, built in 1904, demolished in 1989. (D 582)

scotched this. In the early 1980s, the City marketed the site, but there was little response except from those who wanted the City to relax its control on office building here. Instead the City set up a scheme with a developer whereby English Heritage grant aid was levered in, to make the property developable. The rising price of property meant that the developers made their profit, although the terms of the agreement with English Heritage meant that their grant was repaid. However, as the Planning Department ruefully noted in 1987, 'Inevitably, market forces are pushing the accommodation up-market and the original aspirations of the Local Plan for a balanced housing mix are not being realised'.[17]

Canon's Marsh

The largest area for potential development, and the most difficult, was Canon's Marsh. Divided between three major landowners and a number of smaller stakeholders, and with immense problems of contamination over a large part of it, progress here was slow. The additional difficulty of planning blight by road proposals before 1980 meant an understandable reluctance on anyone's part to devise an approach. In 1979 Federated Land submitted initial proposals for developing part of Canon's Marsh and followed these with a detailed submission in 1980 that included 250,000 sq ft of specialist shopping. The City accepted the scheme, but Federated Land withdrew when it reassessed the profitability of so much shopping. In 1982 the City Council decided to develop its own leisure centre on the site, including a multi-purpose hall and a leisure pool. With political control likely to change, the Labour council rushed ahead with plans and even turned the first sod for the building in May 1983; in June the new Conservative Council cancelled the project, at a cost of £600,000. Then in November 1983 the Council's consultants Hillier-Parker presented a report for the overall development of Canon's Marsh. Its proposals for large-scale office and shopping development conflicted with the Council's established policy, so instead a new brief

Lloyd's Bank high street banking headquarters under construction on the site of the old tobacco bonds. (D 9053)

was issued, proposing an evolutionary approach where each element of development was to be viable in its own right. Initially there was little response from the commercial sector, although the Watershed media complex, complete with Bristol's first commercial radio station, did emerge from this period.

All that changed in 1987. After a period of secretive negotiations with officers of the City Council, Lloyds Bank submitted an application to build their new national high street banking headquarters on Canon's Marsh. Such a large-scale office development clearly conflicted with the brief, but other factors had come into play. There was a widespread and justifiable belief that, if permission were denied, the government would impose an Urban Development Corporation on the city, which would anyway allow Lloyds and many others to build what they wished. Gleefully wrongfooting the Department of the Environment, the City granted Lloyds permission in April, planning officers having extracted what planning gain they could from the situation. The decision was based on some inventive justification;

Square Sail's tall ships at Canon's Marsh, 1988, part of the promotion of the Historic Harbour. (P 14875)

for instance, the Brief opposed large-scale speculative offices, but Lloyds were going to wholly occupy theirs. The development would also remove the concrete tobacco bonds that were considered to be a formidable obstacle to progress in the area. Until this point, Imperial Tobacco had maintained that they were essential to its business, but suddenly they became unnecessary. This may have been connected with Lord Hanson's purchase of IT the year before; as well as being renowned as an asset stripper, Hanson sat on the board of Lloyds. The Conservation Advisory Panel, whilst accepting the inevitability of the process, nevertheless commented that granting planning permission for this scheme in a Conservation Area regrettably 'gave the impression that normal planning principles were not being applied because of the size and economic strength of the applicant'.[18]

By the time of the spectacular demolition of the 1920s concrete warehouses on 29 May 1988, the widely anticipated Urban Development Corporation for Bristol had been announced, but without Canon's Marsh in its portfolio. Instead, and after legal challenges from both local authorities that succeeded in further reducing its operational area, the Bristol Development Corporation (BDC) was focused on St Philips Marsh, Bristol's industrial backyard, and included land alongside the upper reaches of the Floating Harbour, the Feeder Canal and the river Avon, but, significantly, no control of the waterways. Apart from briefly reviving the idea of a barrage on the Avon (their preferred site was just east of Gaol Ferry Bridge on the New Cut) and providing a new footbridge close to Temple Meads the BDC paid little attention to the Harbour, and instead concentrated on improving the road infrastructure into the area. Opinions differ about the success or otherwise of its seven-year reign. Development of its sites bordering the upper Harbour along Temple Back and Avonside Wharf, largely for office use, continues at the time of writing.

As has been observed, 'The grounds for declaring a Bristol UDC appear to reflect the view that the City Council was ill-disposed to development and that the development log-jam in the city could only be freed through an agency which brought with it a private-sector perspective'.[19] Whether that view was deserved or not, the combination of the Lloyds affair and the arrival of the BDC saw changes in the relationship between City Council and business leaders. In June 1987, the three major Canon's Marsh landowners – the City, British Rail and South West Gas – announced a partnership to develop the remainder of the area. The American consultancy LDR was appointed to draw up another vision document for the area, this time including Wapping Wharf on the opposite bank of the Harbour. When they reported back in 1989 with an office-focused plan in the style pioneered by Baltimore showing huge new structures on several key sites, in apparent opposition to their brief, they were told to look again. The revised plan that appeared in 1990 was a slight improvement, for the first time showing a cultural heart to Canon's Marsh, including a major concert hall to replace the Colston Hall, a possibility of a swimming pool and relocation of the successful exhibition centre. Little investment was attracted and it was another three years before the next major step forward.

The Emergence of 'Harbourside'

In 1992, with the persuasion of the Bristol Chamber of Commerce & Initiative the main landowners, this time including Lloyds, got back together and formed the Harbourside Sponsors Group. The new name Harbourside – aestheticism rearing its head again – was a determined gesture to move on from the site's history. It wasn't the first time this had been tried – as early as 1982 the City Docks Group (a small group of Council officers who had been given the task of co-ordinating and reconciling short-term usage with long-term and permanent development in the docks as long back as 1976) had debated reviving the use of Floating Harbour as a name instead of City Docks, and shortly after this the Bristol Marketing Board promoted Bristol's 'Historic Harbour' in a two-year-long campaign. However, more was at stake this time.

The Sponsors Group was broadly in agreement that a cultural heart was needed for Harbourside, but as before, the source of funding was not obvious. However, in 1995, the National Lottery was launched, and Bristol swiftly pulled together a series of linked projects to bid for Lottery and Millennium funding. In 1996 the Millennium Commission awarded £41m towards the creation of Science World (later renamed Explore @ Bristol, a hands-on science centre exploiting the ideas behind Prof Richard Gregory's pioneering Exploratory, and housed in the remodelled GWR goods shed) and Wildscreen World (later Wildwalk, an 'electronic zoo' and IMAX cinema complex envisioned by Chris Parsons, former head of the BBC Natural History Unit based in Bristol, partially housed in the former Rowe Brothers lead works); both projects found favour because of their originality and their roots within the city. At the same time the Arts Council released funds for initial design work for a Centre for the Performing Arts; German architects Benisch & Partners created a world-class 'exploding greenhouse' design overhanging the water's edge. The initial success of these projects went a long way towards consolidating the partnership.

1996 also saw a renewed focus on the water. Understandably the development of the land around the docks had occupied most people's attention during the preceding 20 years but whilst the developments steadily grew, changes had been afloat. The last Bristol-built ship, the Guinness tanker *Miranda Guinness*, had been launched from Charles Hill's yard in 1976 and quietly motored out of the city in 1977, but part of Hill's premises had been taken over by David Abels to build small workboats. Abels' production has been steady ever since (with the occasional hiccough, traditional in an industry always working close to the margin) and some of the vessels that have emerged have rivalled Hill's later productions in size. The neighbouring marina helped to accommodate the steady stream of vessels that arrived at the Harbour, as Bristol became increasingly attractive as a place to live. By the mid-1990s, most long-term moorings had been taken up. Larger vessels also arrived: in 1983 the *Thekla* came to Bristol to begin a career first as a thoroughly unusual theatre and later as

a concert venue and club, a role in which it still thrives. Others were less successful: the *Manx Maid*, a former Isle of Man car ferry, was proposed as a floating conference centre on Wapping Wharf in 1985, but was rejected because of her size. By 1995, both the existing floating pubs, the *Lochiel* and the *Lightship*, were considered to have reached the end of their useful lives and were scrapped. Five years previously,

The sand dredger *Harry Brown* alongside at Poole's Wharf in 1985. (BIM slide 801)

118

the remaining sand importing businesses had been bought up by ARC and their small vessels replaced by more economical large ships. Then in 1991 the trade moved to Avonmouth[20] and the wharf at Hotwells became a housing development, bringing an end to regular shipping traffic in and out of the Harbour.

In 1994, a start was made on a conjectural reconstruction of John Cabot's ship *Matthew*, on which he sailed from Bristol in search of Asia in 1497. The new ship would sail the Atlantic to Newfoundland in 1997 to mark the 500th anniversary of Cabot's rediscovery of North America, and to publicise this, the International Festival of the Sea was staged in Bristol in 1996. In terms of spectacle, the four-day show was stunning, probably assembling more vessels in the Harbour than had ever been there at one time. It says much for the way that Bristol people had adopted the docks as their playground that there was tremendous opposition to charging admission and the security perimeter erected to enable it. It also aroused the spectre of the slave trade; for some, Cabot's voyage of discovery marked the start of imperial ambition that led to the African diaspora and was therefore nothing to celebrate. The hull of the *Matthew* was launched during the Festival and the little ship successfully made the voyage of commemoration in 1997. Since then she has become a familiar sight in the Harbour and regularly attends maritime events in Europe.

In 1998, the Arts Council delivered a bombshell to the confidence of the Harbourside Sponsors Group when it withdrew funding for the Centre for the Performing Arts, causing its abandonment. This was a desperate disappointment. The acrimony that followed was largely aimed at the Arts Council but it was nevertheless damaging for the partners. More trials were to follow. The land to the west of the cultural core of Canon's Marsh was largely privately owned and in 1997 Crest Nicholson had won the competition to develop it. Their scheme aroused opposition when they tabled a plan incorporating a very large leisure centre close to the cathedral. The *Bristol Evening Post*, usually content to sit on the fence, declared it an appalling scheme,[21] and Crest wisely decided to withdraw it. In August 1999

they presented a revised outline that included smaller buildings, a hotel, a multiplex cinema and a swimming pool. This still didn't satisfy the opposition and the introduction of an alternative scheme devised by George Ferguson, a well-known Bristol architect who had been involved in previous battles in the docks since the 1970s, helped to indicate the direction in which the development plans should head. Parts of Ferguson's Little Venice scheme involved the introduction of canals, the abandonment of the leisure centre and the retention of the sole surviving transit shed on the site; this shed mysteriously caught fire and was totally destroyed shortly afterwards.

The Crest scheme was finally considered at an open session of the Planning Committee in February 2000. In scenes redolent of the Colston Hall meeting of 1969, the public gallery of the Council chamber was packed with over 300 people and the proceedings were relayed to still more in an adjacent hall. Over 40 representatives made submissions for and against aspects of the scheme and at the close, despite a guarded recommendation for its acceptance, the Committee voted 7 to 4 against. After further political wrangling, Crest were given one further chance to come up with an acceptable scheme, engaging Edward Cullinan Associates as designers. After much more public consultation, Cullinan's option was finally approved in outline in October 2001 and in detail in February 2004. The first phase was completed in 2006, to mixed reactions, but at the time of writing the final phase has come to a halt as a victim of the slump that began in late 2008.

During the wrangling over Canon's Marsh, other schemes had gone ahead. Small-scale development included the conversion of the 1950s river police station into the riverstation restaurant in 1997, and the remodelling of the oldest surviving dockside transit shed, the Hide or Severn Shed, into Severnshed restaurant in 1999.[22] On western Wapping Wharf, new flats named The Point were built on former railway sidings in 2000 after considerable public consultation. Across the water on Brandon Wharf, the site of the Limekiln Dock and directly opposite the *Great Britain*, more flats appeared; these are arguably the most distinctive in the entire docks area, although where their name,

Capricorn Quay, emerged from is anyone's guess. The Underfall Yard received a welcome boost when a Trust was formed to take on some of the redundant parts and refurbish them for use by the maritime community after 1997. In 2000, the Millennium projects that formed the @ Bristol complex opened to great acclaim[23]. This was accompanied by a comprehensive refocusing of the former Exhibition Centre buildings (U and V Shed, the former being demolished and rebuilt in effigy) into waterside restaurants and bars and the construction of a new footbridge, designed by Irish artist Eilis O'Connell and named for Pero Jones, an enslaved African man brought to Bristol as a servant by John Pinney in 1783. Remodelling of the Tramways Centre diverted the main roads away from the water, and a new pedestrianised area replete with feature waterfall and fountains was created to reflect the previous existence of a waterway here. There were those that believed that the water should have been reinstated, and the rather languid fountains were not to everyone's taste; the then Lord Mayor memorably referred to them as 'like 20 old men peeing in a pond'.[24]

In 2001 the Heritage Lottery Fund pledged £11m towards the development of a history Museum of Bristol to replace the Industrial Museum, and work is currently well advanced on the new museum, due to open in 2011. Behind this is one of only two major sites still awaiting redevelopment in the docks; Wapping Wharf was well advanced and is another victim of the slump. Redcliffe Wharf still awaits a sympathetic scheme. The most significant development at the time of writing is the commitment by the Council to upgrade the machinery that operates the Floating Harbour's lock gates and flood defence gates. Over £11m will be invested over four years, aimed at future-proofing the Harbour in its role as the city's main flood defence and waterway for the next century. The Councillor responsible said 'I want to make sure our multi-million pound improvement works ensures the docks retain their place at the heart of the city's heritage and industrial past and remain a great place to visit and enjoy'[25] – surely a reflection of the status that the Harbour has attained in the last forty years.

1. Bristol City Centre Policy Report 1966
2. Quoted by George Edney at the Colston Hall meeting
3. Wall & Shipsides, 1981
4. Bristol Evening Post 30 September 1968 and subsequent days
5. Bristol City Council Civic News No. 133, August 1969 – 'The Future of the City Docks'
6. Typescript transcription of the meeting BRO 42080
7. For a detailed account of the ship's salvage and arrival in Bristol see Richard Goold-Adams The Return of the Great Britain 1976. Relations have improved since; in the early 1980s the Council constructed the Maritime Heritage Centre as a display centre to help contextualise the ship and in 2000 handed over a long lease on land surrounding the dockyard to allow the Trust to build a development to provide income for the future of the ship
8. Casson Conder & Partners – Bristol City Docks Redevelopment Study 1972
9. op cit p9
10. op cit p5
11. Bristol City Docks Group Report 1 The Opportunities of the Docks, 1974
12. Jenner, M. – 'Bristol Waterfront' in Bristol Illustrated July 1986
13. The Opportunities of the Docks, BCC, 1977
14. op cit
15. Tallon, A. – 'Regenerating Bristol's Harbourside' – Town & Country Planning 1 Oct 2006
16. Quoted in Bristol City Docks Information Pack, 1987
17. Bristol City Docks Information Pack, 1987
18. Conservation Advisory Panel quoted in Punter, 1990. See Punter's book for a masterly survey of the first phase of Harbour redevelopment to 1990.
19. Regeneration Research Summary No. 18, 1998 The Impact of Urban Development Corporations in Leeds, Bristol and Central Manchester
20. Since the early stages of Harbour redevelopment, the sand boats had been encouraged to remain. Bringing building sand into the heart of the city, close to where it was needed, they saved countless lorry movements.
21. BEP 10 March 1999
22. Severn Shed was trumpeted by its owners to be a Brunel design; if so, it is one of the engineer's several posthumous achievements! In fact, it was built in 1863, four years after his death and over a decade after IKB's last involvement with the Harbour.
23. By 2007, Wildwalk and the IMAX cinema had closed, although Explore continues to thrive, and there are plans to turn Wildwalk into an aquarium and to re-open the cinema. It is interesting that the short period since the closure of the Harbour has seen the rise and demise of a number of waterfront cultural venues – Bristol Industrial Museum (1978-2006), the National Lifeboat Museum (1981–1988), the Maritime Heritage Centre (1986-2002), exhibition galleries at Watershed (1983-2002), Radio West (later GWR) (1983-2000).
24. Cllr Bill Martin quoted on BBC Radio Bristol, 14 June 2002
25. Cllr Rosalie Walker quoted in a City Council press release 9 December 2008

Canon's Marsh redevelopment nearing completion in 2007, also showing new housing to the left of the Gas works and to the south of the Harbour. (PM slide 45)

9 CONCLUSION

The Floating Harbour as we see it today is the product of a prolonged period of human intervention in the way that the two rivers, the Avon and the Frome, flow through Bristol. It is a story of continuity and change. The basic shape of the Harbour, together with the New Cut, has remained much the same since the works of 1804-09, although within the Harbour the margins between the water and the land have been subject to considerable change: dry docks and slipways have come and gone, and naturally sloping river banks have been turned into vertical stone walls. The water itself, once heavily polluted by sewage and industrial effluent, is now much cleaner. Around the waterside virtually all the buildings have been either replaced or recycled into new uses in the last 30 years. Some iconic landmark buildings such as the Bush Warehouse, the Watershed and Buchanan's Wharf remain, albeit converted to entirely different uses.

'Penny steamers' carried passengers around the Harbour, this one pictured at Bathurst Wharf in the 1930s. (P 12270)

From an earlier era the nearby churches of St Stephen and St Mary Redcliffe still feature in many modern images of the harbour, as they have done for centuries.

Two hundred years after its construction the Floating Harbour remains a very visible and significant part of the urban landscape of central Bristol, although its history as a working port is becoming less and less evident. Nevertheless, the Floating Harbour stands as a striking tribute to the Rev William Milton's visionary plan and to William Jessop's interpretation and implementation of Milton's idea. Enormous credit is due to these creators of the Floating Harbour, and to later engineers such as I K Brunel, Thomas Howard, John Girdlestone and J M McCurrich who refined and developed the concept, without ever needing to challenge its basic integrity. The Floating Harbour became a conservation area in 1979, and while this designation has not prevented extensive redevelopment it has undoubtedly helped to preserve the historic character of the area. The valuable heritage status of the Floating Harbour is signalled by the City Council's commitment to spending £11million repairing and preserving it.

Looking at the whole history of the Floating Harbour, we can see that at first the engineering triumph was almost an economic and financial disaster, rescued eventually by the growth of the global economy and Britain's dominance of international trade in the second half of the nineteenth century. In the twentieth century the City Docks reached their peak just before the First World War and never fully recovered thereafter. Nevertheless the PBA continued to invest and the Docks remained economically viable until the late 1960s, when wider economic and technological change combined to bring about their demise. It is the slowness, and yet the relentlessness, of change that is apparent over this long period. As we noted in chapter 2, there was a very long period of debate and prevarication before a sufficiently broad body of local opinion concluded that something had to be done to improve the harbour. Once it was built there was then another prolonged period of what might be called wilful inactivity by the Dock Company, before the takeover by the Town Council in 1848 opened the way for a series of improvements – extending the quays and bringing in the railway. In another indicator of the slowness of change we saw in chapter 5 that sail- and steam-powered ships co-existed for more than half a century. In the same way, the Floating Harbour carried on successfully operating alongside the two river-mouth docks at Portishead and Avonmouth for many years after they were opened in the late 1870s. If the closure of the City Docks in the twentieth century now looks to have been inevitable we should remember that this was not how it looked to those involved, for the PBA and its private sector partners went on investing right up to the mid-1960s.

By comparison with these slow changes, the final demise of the Docks in the 1970s was remarkably sudden, and this may account for some of the subsequent dereliction and delay in implementing plans for regeneration. Another factor was the politically contentious nature of plans for the future use of the Docks – in a sense this was a re-run of the prolonged debate about how to improve the rivers in the eighteenth century, with different interests thwarting progress by presenting competing visions of the best way forward.

No longer a working port, the Floating Harbour has been transformed from a state of depressing dereliction in the late 1970s to its current shiny vibrancy by a combination of civic and private enterprise. This can also be seen as a continuation of the tradition of partnership between Council and port users over many years. While the City Council, as the planning authority and a major landowner, has established the guidelines for change, businesses both big and small have made their distinctive contributions – from the Crest Nicholson redevelopment of Canon's Marsh to Brunel's Buttery, the vendor of famously tasty bacon sandwiches at Prince's Wharf. If it feels to Bristolians to have taken a long time, the scale of the transformation needs to be remembered for it is more dramatic than anything in the preceding history of the port. Although some people were already

Ferry boat *Margaret*, the first of the revived ferries in the 1970s, at work in 2007. (photo courtesy of the Bristol Ferry Boat Company)

using the Harbour for leisure activities well before its commercial closure, and the potential for further development was perceived at an early stage, the extent of dereliction was daunting, and it is only now that the renovation of all waterside sites is nearing completion. In one important sense Bristol's rather slow and faltering progress may have turned out for the best: if the 1969 scheme had gone ahead and large parts of the Floating Harbour had been 'reclaimed' then the city would have lost the opportunity to make the water a centrepiece of urban regeneration. In the event other places, notably Baltimore in the United States, pioneered the recycling of redundant docks, and port cities around the world have subsequently found their own ways of transforming their old docks areas into fashionable and successful twenty-first century urban spaces.

In the Bristol version of dockland regeneration the predominant new land uses are residential, leisure and culture, centred around a conservation ethic, in contrast to Baltimore where a vast amount of commercial office space replaced dock buildings that had been completely cleared away. There is some office development around the Floating Harbour, but apart from the bank buildings at Canon's Marsh and a solicitors' office upstream from Bristol Bridge, the waterside buildings, whether newly constructed or renovated, are mainly for homes. Baltimore provided a pioneering example of successful docklands regeneration and served as a model and inspiration for many cities facing up to the same sort of problem. It showed that it was not only possible to regenerate rundown docks but also that such places could be made attractive to 'high tech' service industries (including banking and the law) and tourists. The regeneration of Bristol's Floating Harbour has successfully followed a 'second way' that did not involve large-scale speculative commercial development, and that was considered impossible to achieve by developers. The Bristol docks regeneration is also notably well integrated into the city as a whole.

It is almost as if the Floating Harbour stands as a metaphor for change in Britain in that it used to be a bustling port in the days of British economic ascendancy and now it epitomises the importance of financial services and tourism exploiting the urban heritage left after the decline of the old manufacturing and trading economy. The *Great Britain* does this on its own: once a symbol of Britain's leading role in maritime engineering and enterprise it is now, in exactly the same dry dock from which it was launched in 1843, the leading heritage attraction for visitors to the Floating Harbour. In the case of the Floating Harbour regeneration has created what might be called primarily a consumption space. In other words, an area that was previously dominated by trade and industry is now predominantly about the activities of people as consumers, whether as residents or visitors. The prominence of housing schemes around the waterside is also a reminder of a wider pattern of change, which has seen falling levels of employment in city centres and rising amounts of residential development. Governments around the world are keen to increase urban residential densities and we can be pretty confident that there are now more people living close to the Floating Harbour than was ever the case when it was a working port. Moreover, the distinctly up-market character of much of the new waterside housing may be seen as signalling a marked change from the low-wage economy that prevailed in the days of the working port. There was never a clear-cut

and distinctive dockland neighbourhood around the Floating Harbour and so it is not the case that in the new developments middle-class professionals have driven out the local working classes. Nevertheless, despite the best efforts of the Council to achieve a balance of housing, the exclusiveness of these developments does mean that for the majority of Bristolians the Floating Harbour is a place they can visit but not live in.

The people of Bristol are strongly attached to the Floating Harbour, making abundant use of it, in all sorts of ways, whether walking beside it or sailing on it. They flock in huge numbers to regular events such as the annual Harbour Festival. In an era of increasing urban densities the retention of stretches of open water may be seen as a valuable environmental asset, and it is clear that water in cities is very popular with both residents and visitors. Indeed the Floating Harbour is increasingly essential to the drainage and flood protection of Bristol in this age of rising sea levels and climate change, and its value to the overall ecology of the city is only now being fully appreciated.

Looking to the future of the Floating Harbour, the evidence of the past 200 years is that predictions are very risky, but it seems certain that the recent wave of investment has established a pattern of land use for the next 50 to 100 years. In the same way that the survival of the city centre port reflected the commitment of eighteenth-century merchants to building the Floating Harbour to preserve their pre-existing dense social and economic networks, we now see that having made the fateful decision to close the City Docks in the 1970s the Council set out on a new path, which will shape and influence, if not determine, what happens to the Floating Harbour over the coming years. In truth the closure of the Docks in 1975 and the handover of responsibility by the Docks Committee was a much more important historical milestone than the 200th anniversary of the construction of the Floating Harbour. But 2009 does provide a good vantage point not only to reflect on Bristol's maritime heritage but also to assess the emerging character and direction of travel for the Floating Harbour in the years to come.

Dinghy sailors and rowing clubs long ago pioneered leisure uses of the Harbour. Here Bristol Corinthians sail in the Reach, 1962. (Day B1)

Bibliography

Anon (1945) *English City: the growth and future of Bristol*, Bristol: JS Fry Ltd

Atkinson, BJ (1987) 'an Early Example of the Decline of the Industrial Spirit? Bristol 'Enterprise' in the First Half of the Nineteenth Century' *Southern History*, vol. 9, pp71-89

Bagwell and Armstrong, (1988) 'Coastal Shipping', chapter 5 in Freeman and Aldcroft,

Barry, J (2000) 'South West' in Clark

K Bassett, and A Hoare, (1984) 'Bristol and the saga of Royal Portbury: a case study in local politics and municipal enterprise' *Political Geography Quarterly*, vol. 3, no. 3, July, pp223-250

Belcham, J (ed) (2006) *Liverpool 800: culture, character and history*, Liverpool: Liverpool University Press

Benbrook, I (1989) *Bristol City Docks*, Bristol: Redcliffe Press

Bird, J (1963) *The Major Sea Ports of the United Kingdom*, London: Hutchinson

Bristol Broadsides (1983) *Bristol's Other History*, Bristol: Bristol Broadsides

Buchanan, R A (!969) 'The Construction of the Floating Harbour in Bristol: 1804-1809' *Transactions of the Bristol and Gloucestershire Archaeological Society*, vol. LXXXVIII, pp184-204(1969)

-(1969) 'The Cumberland Basin, Bristol' *Industrial Archaeology*, vol. 6, part 4pp 325-333

-(1970) 'IK Brunel and the Port of Bristol' *Transactions of the Newcomen Society*, vol 42, pp41-56

-(1971) *Nineteenth Century Engineers in the Port of Bristol*, Bristol: Bristol Branch of the Historical Association

-(2002) *Brunel: the life and times of Isambard Kingdom Brunel*, London: Hambledon & London

Buchanan, R A and Cossons, N (eds) (1969) *The Industrial Archaeology of the Bristol Region*, Newton Abbott: David and Charles

Buchanan RA & Williams, M (2005) *Brunel's Bristol*, Bristol: Redcliffe Press

Bullock, A (1960) *The Life and Times of Ernest Bevin, vol 1*, London: Heinemann

Burton, A (1994) *The Rise and Fall of British Shipbuilding*, London: Constable

Bush, G (1976) *Bristol and Its Municipal Government 1820-1851*, Bristol: Bristol Record Society

Channon, G (1985) *Bristol and the Promotion of the Great Western Railway*, Bristol: Bristol Branch of the Historical Association

Clark, P (ed) (2000) *The Cambridge Urban History of Britain, vol II*, Cambridge: Cambridge University Press

Daunton, M (ed) (2000) *The Cambridge Urban History of Britain, vol III*, Cambridge: Cambridge University Press

Dresser, M (2007) *Slavery Obscured: the social history of the slave trade in Bristol*, Bristol: Redcliffe Press (first published in 2001)

Dresser, M and Ollerenshaw, P (eds) (1996) *The Making of Modern Bristol*, Bristol: Redcliffe Press

Elkin, P (1995) *Images of Maritime Bristol*, Breedon Books

Elkin, P (2000) 'Old Docks - New Problems at the Port of Bristol 1945-1965' in P Harris (ed) Bristol Branch of the Historical Association

Farr, G (1977) *Shipbuilding in the Port of Bristol*, London: Trustees of the National Maritime Museum

Fischer, L and Jarvis, A (eds) (1999) *Harbours and Havens: essays in port history in honour of Gordon Jackson*, St Johns, Newfoundland: International Maritime Economic History Association

Freeman, M and Aldcroft, D (eds) (1988) *Transport in Victorian Britain*, Manchester: Manchester University Press

Gibson, C (2002) *Bristol's Merchants and the GWR*, Bristol: Bristol branch of the Historical Association

Hadfield, C and Skempton, A (1979) *William Jessop, Engineer*, Newton Abbott: David and Charles

Harley, C (1971) 'The shift from sailing ships to steamships, 1850-1890: a study in technological change and diffusion' in McCloskey, D (ed) *Essays on a mature Economy: Britain after 1840*, London Methuen

Harvey, C and Press, J (eds) (1988) *Studies in the Business History of Bristol*, Bristol: Bristol Academic Press

Hasegawa, J (1992) *Replanning the Blitzed City Centre: a comparative study of Bristol, Coventry and Southampton 1941-1950*, Buckingham: Open University Press

Hyde, F (1971) *Liverpool and the Mersey: the development of a port 1700-1970*, Newton Abbott: David and Charles

Inwood, S (1998) *A History of London*, Basingstoke: Macmillan

Jackson, G (1983) *The History and Archaeology of Ports*, Tadworth: World's Work Ltd

-(1988) 'The Ports' in Freeman and Aldcroft

-(2000) 'Ports, 1700-1840' in Clark, P

Jarvis, A (1999) '*Port History: some thoughts on where it came from and where it might be going'* in Fishcer and Jarvis

Jenner, M (2000) in *Post-war Bristol 1945-65*, Bristol: Bristol Branch of the Historical Association

Jones, P (1989) *Canon's Marsh: the rise and fall of the tobacco bonds*, Redcliffe Press

Kelly, A & Kelly, M (eds) (2006) *Brunel: in love with the impossible*, Bristol: Bristol Cultural Development Partnership

Kelly, K (2001) *The Port of Bristol, 1919-1939: a study of a municipally owned port*, PhD thesis, UWE, Bristol

Langton, J (2000) 'Urban growth and economic change: from the late seventeenth century to 1841' in Clark, Large, D (1984) *The Port of Bristol 1848-1884*, Bristol: Bristol Record Society

Latimer, J (1903) *The History of the Society of Merchant Venturers of the City of Bristol*, Bristol: Arrowsmith

-(1902) *The Annals of Bristol in the Nineteenth Century*, Bristol: William George's & Son

-(1893) *The Annals of Bristol in the Eighteenth Century*, Bristol: Privately published

Little, B (1954) *The City and County of Bristol*, London: Warner Laurie Longmore, J (2006) 'Civic Liverpool: 1680-1800' in Belcham

Lord, J & Southam, J (1983) *The Floating Harbour: a landscape history of the Bristol City Docks*, Bristol: Redcliffe Press

MacInnes, C.M.(1968) *Bristol a gateway of empire,* Newton Abbott: David and Charles (first published 1939)

- (1962) *Bristol at War*, London: Museum Press

Mathias, P (1983) *The First Industrial Nation,* London: Routledge

McGrath, P (1972) (ed) *Bristol in the Eighteenth Century*, Newton Abbott: David and Charles

- (1975) *The Merchant Venturers of Bristol*, Bristol: Society of Merchant Venturers

McGrath, P and Cannon, J (eds) (1976) *Essays in Bristol and Gloucestershire History*, Bristol: Bristol and Gloucestershire Archaeological Society

Milne, G (1999) 'Port politics: interest, faction and port management in mid-Victorian Liverpool' in Fischer and Jarvis

- (2006) 'Maritime Liverpool' in Belcham

Minchinton, W (1962) (ed) *The Port of Bristol in the eighteenth century*, Bristol: Historical Association

- (1972) 'The port of Bristol in the eighteenth century' in McGrath

Morgan, K, (1993) *Bristol and the Atlantic Trade in the Eighteenth Century*, Cambridge: Cambridge University Press

- (1996) 'The Economic Development of Bristol, 1700-1850' in Dresser and Ollerenshaw

Murphy B (1973) *A History of the British Economy 1086-1970*, London: Longman

Neale, W G (1968) *At the Port of Bristol, vol I: members and problems, 1848-1914,* Bristol: Port of Bristol Authority

-(1970) *At the port of Bristol. Vol.II. The turn of the tide 1900-1914,* Bristol: Port of Bristol Authority

-(1976) *The tides of war and the port of Bristol, vol III, 1914-1918,* Bristol: Port of Bristol Authority

Nicholls, J and Taylor, J (1882) *Bristol Past and Present, vol III*, Bristol: Arrowsmith

Ollerenshaw, P & Wardley, P (1996), 'Economic growth and the business community in Bristol since 1840' in Dresser and Ollerenshaw

Palmer, S (2000) 'Ports' in Daunton

Penny, J (1995) *Luftwaffe Operations over Bristol 1940/44,* Bristol: Bristol Branch of the Historical Association

- (2002) *Bristol at War*, Derby: Breedon Books,

Pepys, S (1906) *The Diary of Samuel Pepys*, London: Macmillan

Punter, J (1990) *Design Control in Bristol 1940-1990*, Bristol: Redcliffe Press

Ralph, E, (1973) *Government of Bristol 1373-1973*, Bristol: Bristol City Council

Reid, H (2005) *Bristol Under Siege*, Bristol: Redcliffe Press

Reid, WN and Hicks WE (1877) *Leading events in the history of the port of Bristol,* Bristol: Hemmons

Shipsides, F & Wall, R (1981) *Bristol: maritime city,* Bristol: Redcliffe Press

- *(1992) Quayside Bristol the city and its port in recent years,* Bristol: Redcliffe Press

Shannon, H A & Grebenik, E (1943) *The Population of Bristol*, Cambridge: Cambridge University Press

Stone, G (1909) *Bristol as it was and as it is*, Bristol: Walter Reid

Vincent, M (1979) *Lines to Avonmouth*, Oxford: Oxford Publishing

Wells, C (1909) *A Short History of the Port of Bristol*, Bristol: Arrowsmith

White, K (2006) *A Celebration of the Avon New Cut*, Bristol: Fiducia Press

White, J (2007) *London in the Nineteenth Century*, London: Jonathan Cape

- (2008) *London in the Twentieth Century*, London: Vintage

Whitfield, B (1983) 'Trade unionism in Bristol, 1910-1926', in Bristol Broadsides

Whyte, WH (1934) *Decasualisation of Dock Labour*, Bristol: Arrowsmith

Williams, AF (1962) 'Bristol Port Plans and Improvement Schemes of the 18th Century' *Transactions of the Bristol and Gloucestershire Archaeological Society*, vol. 81, pp 138-181

A Pictorial Survey of the Floating Harbour

This series of illustrations starts at Cumberland Basin, through which most incoming ships would have entered the Floating Harbour. It then moves systematically around the Harbour and up the Feeder Canal to Netham Lock connection to the Avon. It was impossible to construct such a sequence to illustrate the Harbour at one point in time. However, anyone travelling around the Harbour, either on the water or on land, will find interesting historical comparisons.

Aerial view from 1946, showing Cumberland Basin, with Merchants' Dock just beyond, the New Cut to the right, crossed by the Ashton Swing Bridge, the two bonded warehouses and the timber yards at Baltic Wharf between the river and the Harbour. The original course of the river through the site of the Underfall Yard is easy to trace. (PBA 1048)

The centre of attention in this picture from 1929 is the Underfall Yard, in the left foreground, next to the sheds on the timber yards and above the New Cut. The Cumberland Basin junction locks are clearly visible, crossed by the road to the left and the harbour railway to the left. The railway snakes past the top of Merchants' Dock (which had been partly filled to accommodate the railway). To the right of the Dock is Stothert's Shipyard. (PBA 342)

A print of Stothert's shipyard at Poole's Wharf in the nineteenth century, with Merchants' Dock in the foreground and the Floating Harbour beyond. The large dry dock is still visible today. (D 9067)

The *Wanderer*, immortalised in a poem by John Masefield, passing Albion Dockyard and the Baltic Wharf timber yards in 1931, seen from the Mardyke side. (P 9481)

Aerial view of the City Docks, October 1955, showing part of Bathurst Basin, bottom left, with the newly rebuilt L and M Sheds just above. The light coloured area towards the middle of the foreground is the Grove after removal of war damaged buildings. In the middle of the picture the Canon's Marsh railway goods yard is clearly visible, with the Gas Works beyond. The truncated St Augustine's Reach stretches towards the right of the picture. (PBA N622)

Canon's Marsh Gas Works in about 1955, with a vessel at the jetty. Note the un-walled bank at that point, the last remaining stretch of 'natural' river bank within the Harbour. Passing the Gas Works, which was established in 1824, is the railway line into the Canon's Marsh Goods Yard, visible at the top of the picture. At the bottom can be seen lines of trucks on the Wapping Railway Wharf. (D 10075)

Wapping Railway Wharf in about 1905, looking east, with the Corporation Granary top left. (D 9262)

The French ship *Leoville* berthed at Z Shed, Canon's Marsh, June 1952, with a steam engine visible to the right. (PBA 1835)

Prince's Wharf in June 1938, a scene dominated by the bulk of the Corporation Granary (destroyed by a bomb in 1941). To the right can be seen the Fairbairn 35-ton steam crane, and behind it the Guinness Shed. (PBA 794)

The view up St Augustine's Reach from the top of the Granary about 1900. The recently completed sheds, known as T, V and U, line the left bank, with no sign of cranes to assist the task of unloading ships. On the right are the longer established Narrow Quay and the Bush Warehouse (built in the 1830s). (D 654)

St Augustine's Reach looking downstream from the Stone Bridge over the river Frome, early 1890s, shortly before this part of the Harbour was covered over to form what is now Colston Avenue. St Stephen's church tower stands, as always, to the left, and the classical façade of St Mary-on-the-Quay is to the right. By this stage few vessels made the journey to the upper part of the Harbour past the drawbridge, which can be seen in the middle of the picture. (D 9531)

This aerial shot from the 1960s shows the rebuilt L and M Sheds, with the well stocked Wapping coal yard behind. The original buildings on the Bathurst Basin side of Wapping Road are still standing. Above them can be seen the Bathurst Basin entrance lock and a length of the New Cut. (D 10418)

Bathurst Basin in 1939, with the General Hospital in the background and the entrance lock gates in the foreground. The ships are sand dredgers from the Holms fleet that used the Basin as their base until 1980. (PBA 912)

This view of the Harbour from Prince Street bridge, with the eighteenth-century houses of Redcliffe Parade and the spire of St Mary Redcliffe has been recorded many times over the years, but here we have the scene as it appeared in 1937. Cranes are unloading a ship moored at the Grove while a tug journeys downstream with two empty barges. (PBA 776)

In 1871 the view from the top of St Mary Redcliffe church shows not only the volume of shipping using the harbour above Prince Street Bridge but also (at the extreme left) Bathurst Wharf under construction, and two of the earliest quayside sheds on the Grove, including the extant Severn Shed. There is only one steamer in the entire picture. (D 9710)

This shows the distinctive character of Redcliffe Back, where large buildings front directly onto the water. Grain storage and flour milling dominated this stretch for more than half a century, but by 1937 when this picture was taken most activity had already moved to Avonmouth. (PBA 688)

Ships crowd the quayside in this picture of Welsh Back in 1875. The skyline is dominated by the bulk of the Granary (built in 1869), with the spire of St Nicholas's church on the extreme right. (D 10421)

Bristol Bridge from Welsh Back, before November 1940, showing Bridge Street beyond. The bridge was effectively the limit of the Harbour for sea-going vessels, but cargoes were regularly carried further upstream by barges. (Pos 248)

Back of Bridge Street from the river above Bristol Bridge in 1921. All of these buildings were destroyed or severely damaged by bombs aimed at the docks in November and December 1940. Note the 'penny steamers' for pleasure trips and the headquarters of the Redcliffe Rowing Club – evidence of early leisure use of the Harbour. (P 13848)

George's Brewery (later Courage's) above Bristol Bridge, in September 1920. The mast of the trow (a traditional Bristol Channel sailing barge) could easily be lowered to return through the bridge. (P 13711)

These massive buildings upstream from the Brewery had been part of Finzel's sugar refinery before being used as Bennett Bros printing works. At the time this photograph was taken in 1920 they were derelict, but they were not demolished until 1929. (P 13712)

In the foreground of this photograph from 1899 work is going on to construct the Counterslip electricity generating station for Bristol's tram system. On the far bank are industrial buildings and the backs of buildings in Castle Street, later destroyed by bombing in 1940-41. (D 474)

Avon Street wharf just above St Philip's bridge in 1922, with the glass cone of the Phoenix works, Bristol's last glassworks that would close the following year. Christopher Thomas's Broad Plain soap works can be seen in the distance. This stretch of the Harbour served Bristol's industrial back yard. (P 13765)

Midland Railway Wharf, Avon Street, June 1898, showing cranes moving cargo from barges to railway trucks. The opposition of the Great Western Railway meant that the Midland only ever reached the Harbour at this point. The large cones are part of Powell and Ricketts glassworks. (D 2249)

John Lysaght's galvanising works on the Feeder Canal, 1920. As this picture shows, the Feeder was much more than a water supply for the Harbour, providing Lysaght's, the Great Western Cotton Factory, the Netham Alkali Works, St Annes Board Mill and William Butler's tar works with a direct route for goods carried in barges to and from ships berthed at the quays below Bristol Bridge. (P 13761)

William Butler's chemical barge *Carbolate* passing through Netham Lock, going into the river Avon, in 1962. On the skyline can be seen two recently completed blocks of flats at Barton Hill, hidden by the recently landscaped former spoil tip of the Netham Alkali Works. On the extreme left is the Great Western cotton factory. (PBA N2981)

Index